FUN ON THE RIVIERA

FODOR'S

FUN ON THE RIVIERA

Published by
Fodor's Travel Publications Inc
New York and London

Copyright © 1988 by Fodor's Travel Publications, Inc.

All rights reserved under International and Pan-American Copyright Conventions. Published in the United States by Fodor's Travel Publications, Inc., a subsidiary of Random House Inc., New York, and simultaneously in Canada by Random House of Canada Limited, Toronto. Distributed by Random House, Inc., New York.

ISBN 0–679–01359–8
ISBN 0–340–40054–4 (Hodder and Stoughton edition)

First Edition

New titles in the series

Barbados
Jamaica

also available

Acapulco
Bahamas
Disney World & the Orlando Area
Las Vegas
London
Maui
New Orleans
New York City
Paris
Rio
St. Martin/St. Maarten
San Francisco
Waikiki

Contents

Map of the Riviera viii-ix

Overview	1
Riviera Briefing	9
General Information *National Tourist Offices, Prices, Climate, Time Zones, Entry and Customs, Getting There and Around, Hotels and Restaurants, Tipping, Shopping, Tax Refunds*	9
St.-Tropez *Map of St.-Tropez* 25	21
Mandelieu-La Napoule	37
Cannes *Map of Cannes* 49	45
Antibes and Juan-les-Pins *Map of Antibes and Juan-les-Pins* 65	63
Nice *Map of Nice* 85	82
Monaco *Map of Monaco* 109	105
Menton	119
Index	127

Map of Riviera

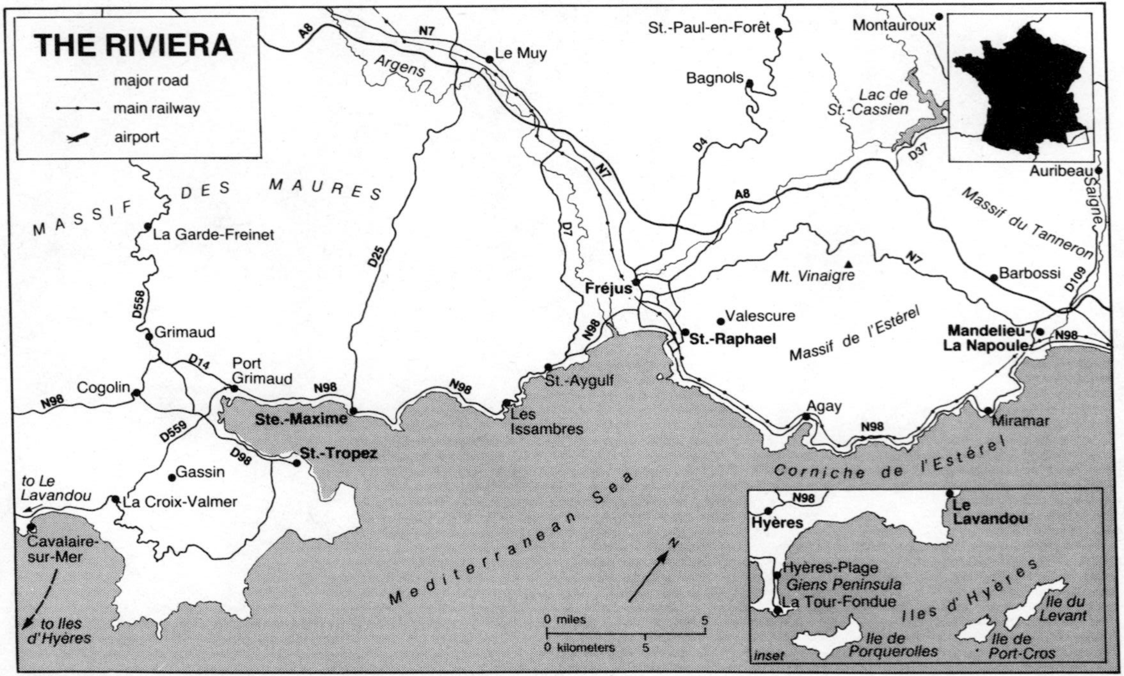

see inset right

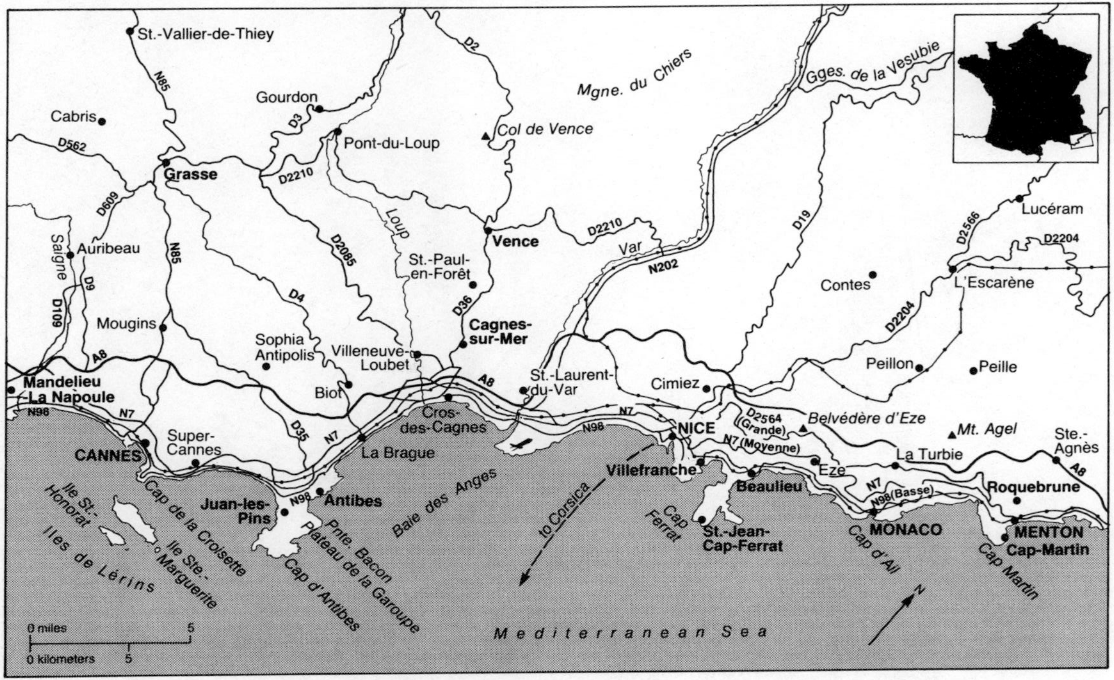
St.-Vallier-de-Thiey
Mgne. du Chiers
Gges. de la Vesubie
Gourdon
Cabris
Col de Vence
Pont-du-Loup
Grasse
Loup
Vence
Var
Lucéram
L'Escarène
Auribeau
Saigne
St.-Paul-en-Forêt
Contes
Mougins
Sophia Antipolis
Cagnes-sur-Mer
Villeneuve-Loubet
Peillon
Peille
Mandelieu-La Napoule
Biot
St.-Laurent-du-Var
Cimiez
Belvédère d'Eze
Mt. Agel
Super-Cannes
Cros-des-Cagnes
NICE
Ste.-Agnès
CANNES
La Brague
La Turbie
Villefranche
Eze
Beaulieu
Roquebrune
Juan-les-Pins
Antibes
Baie des Anges
to Corsica
Cap Ferrat
St.-Jean-Cap-Ferrat
MONACO
MENTON
Cap-Martin
Ile St.-Honorat
Cap de la Croisette
Ile Ste.-Marguerite
Iles de Lérins
Pnte. Bacon
Plateau de la Garoupe
Cap d'Antibes
Cap d'Ail
Cap Martin
Mediterranean Sea
N
0 miles 5
0 kilometers 5
N85
D2
D3
D562
D2210
D609
D2085
D4
D9
D109
D36
N202
D19
D2566
D2204
A8
N98
N7
D35
D2564 (Grande)
N7 (Moyenne)
N98 (Basse)

Overview

The Riviera is a strip of rocky coast on a tideless sea, a sea around which, a few thousand years ago, Western civilization began. Ancient Greeks, raised on tales of Odysseus and his voyages, sailed here and founded colonies and trading posts such as Nicaea, today Nice, and Antipolis, today Antibes. Phoenicians, from the region which is now Lebanon, followed, and around the 4th century B.C. the Celts invaded, to be defeated by the Romans who then took over the area.

For centuries most of the inhabitants of the strip were fishermen, and peasants who grew wheat and olives, and grapes for wine. This was not one of those lush regions of France where the living was easy. There were no palaces or gracious châteaux, only small villages, with fortifications here and there for use when Celts, Vandals, Ostrogoths, Saracens, and pirates from Algeria's Barbary Coast were on the rampage.

Then, in the middle of the last century, Europe's aristocracy fell in love with the Riviera's balmy winter climate. A troupe of kings and queens (including Victoria and dozens of her relations), Russian grand dukes, princelings from obscure Balkan countries, English *milords*, and a rabble of *nouveau riche* camp followers began to make prolonged visits. They had mansions built, and paid for parks and flower gardens to be laid out. Luxury hotels sprang up in imitation of their palaces back home, and, to make sure that their souls didn't suffer while on vacation, they subsidized Anglican churches and Russian cathedrals—the former in the best possible Victorian Gothic taste, the latter gleaming with onion domes and icons.

The newcomers called the coastal strip the French Riviera. The French name for it is la Côte d'Azur, the blue—literally sky-blue—coast. To the French, the word "Riviera" refers to the Italian coast farther east.

All these rich invaders withdrew to the cooler north for the summer months. No person of quality, and above all no lady of quality, would risk getting tanned like the unfortunate peasants. Until World War II many hotels closed at the end of May, reopening in October. Hoteliers and key staff migrated north to open other establishments along the Channel coast, at Deauville and Dinard, for the summer season.

In those days, fun on the Riviera was sedate, apart from a few scandalous liaisons conducted discreetly behind closed doors. There was gossip over the tea table, and gentle strolls along civilized sidewalks (the English colony paid for the promenade des Anglais at Nice) and among the ornamental trees and phalanxed flowerbeds of the public gardens. There was even the occasional flutter at Monte Carlo, where Monaco's crumbling economy was buttressed by the creation of the casino, strictly for foreigners only. But one thing there was very little of was sea bathing, except as a drastic medical remedy—the brutal immersion prescribed by doctors with strong ideas on hydrotherapy.

Then came the fun revolution. In the '20s and '30s people began to like it hot. It was no more than a scattering of writers and artists at first, but the rest of the world wasn't far behind. Sun, sea, and sex . . . The peasantry of the West were now pale factory and office workers, and their badge of leisure and pleasure became the tan that their aristocratic predecessors had so assiduously avoided.

More and more hotels, restaurants, and nightclubs were built. Now, of course, the hotels no longer closed down in July and August—they stayed open and put their prices up. A few even began to close in winter, the old high season. Texan and Saudi oil billionaires gave the kiss of life to the vast palace hotels that had survived two world wars. Fun became livelier and more informal. Toplessness, and even bottomlessness, arrived on the beaches. Campsites opened to accommodate the relatively poor who wanted to sample the fabled hedonistic life.

So popular has the Riviera become today, that anyone who loves peace and solitude should seek out the inland country with its picturesque hilltop villages, and even the gregarious should think twice about braving the coast-loving crowds of July and August. But, these considerations apart, fun on the Riviera is now available in most forms to most people in a widely varied range of Mediterranean resorts from St.-Tropez in the west to Menton on the Italian border.

HIGHLIGHTS AND FUN CENTERS

The Riviera is a demi-paradise for those in love with its sparkling sea, red rocks, and charming inland villages. The rich rejoice that most of the pleasures money can buy are so conveniently and lavishly available. The not-so-rich can enjoy the scenery, climate, and ambience of the area—and perhaps indulge in a brief bout of high luxury from time to time.

Traveling from west to east, the climate becomes warmer. The Mistral—that dreaded north wind that sweeps down the Rhône valley, bending trees and souring tempers at Aix-en-Provence—can sometimes be a nuisance at St.-Tropez, the most westerly outpost of the Riviera, but at Menton, it is just something to read about in a newspaper as you relax under a lemon tree.

The beaches are sandy from St.-Tropez to Antibes, about midway along the coast. From there on they are

INTRODUCING THE RIVIERA

rocky, though some sand has been thoughtfully spread at Menton and Monaco. Private beaches are everywhere, and these you must pay to use, but you do get value for money—a mattress and parasol, a café or restaurant, and the pleasure of watching the perpetual parade of stylish swimwear and languid egos.

The entire coastline can be regarded as one gigantic fun center, but it does have seven specific focal points, which are listed below with brief notes on the particular pleasures each has to offer. Later in the book, each has a chapter devoted to it. Between these centers lie both the bastions of privilege and exclusivity, where the villas of the super-rich stand in extensive private grounds, and, in complete contrast, those lesser resorts which are more suitable for family vacations. The dramatically beautiful inland country is touched on only briefly—it is not really part of the subject of the book, but on the other hand it has some good hotels, magnificent views, lots of local color, and no Riviera holiday would be complete without at least one excursion into it.

● St.-Tropez

St.-Tropez was just a small picturesque fishing port until it was "discovered" in the '50s by the beautiful people—the film stars, the starlets, the "fast set"—and by others who scorned bourgeois values while enjoying bourgeois bank balances. This is a town of top hotels, restaurants, and nightclubs, of chic little shops, and of immense gleaming yachts. Conspicuous consumption could hardly be more conspicuous than it is here. The place can be quite informal, but it's an expensive and deliberate kind of informality.

St.-Tropez is 43 miles from the next major resort—the hills of the Massif des Maures and the Massif de l'Estérel lie between it and Mandelieu-La Napoule, which can be reached by car via the horribly overcrowded coast road or, for those in funds, by helicopter.

● Mandelieu-La Napoule

Mandelieu-La Napoule, which is made up of two merged villages, may not be one of the legendary Riviera resorts, but it has recently been developed as an excellent sporting center, backed up by several good restaurants, one of which ranks in the world's top twenty. Anyone whose ideal vacation is spent windsurfing, sailing, playing tennis, or enjoying any number of other outdoor activities, will find it very much to their taste. The only drawback is that it's difficult to reach without a car.

● **Cannes**
Cannes comes next, as you progress in an easterly direction. This is *the* elegant resort *par excellence*. Created by foreign wealth in the last century, and unceasingly modernized since, it boasts palatial hotels and world famous festivals: high life with a vengeance. There's always something going on. Unlike most other Riviera resorts, it creates occasions upon which a gentleman will discover that he needs to wear a jacket and tie. Indeed, it is not uncommon to spot tuxedos and—weather permitting—mink coats in Cannes.

● **Antibes/Juan-les-Pins**
Antibes and Juan-les-Pins are six or seven miles along the coast and, like Mandelieu-La Napoule, the two original villages form one town now. Juan-les-Pins is the modern part, with an intense nightlife; Antibes is older, a small town with an integrity of its own, whose narrow streets, markets, and castles were there long before tourism began.

● **Nice**
Nice is next, on the other side of the Baie des Anges. It's a big city, the capital of the Riviera, with a population of 338,000, industries, a university, and many residents who lead lives entirely unconnected with tourism. However, it has luxuries to match or beat Cannes, as well as inexpensive places to stay and to eat. It's also the transport center of the Riviera, not only because of its airport—the third busiest in France after Orly and Charles de Gaulle in Paris—but because it is well served by buses and trains. Even the expresses stop here, and you can catch a train to anywhere else on the coast (except St.-Tropez, out on its limb). You can even take a boat over to Corsica

should you feel inclined to discover a totally different way of life.

● **Monaco**
Monaco lies about ten miles east along the coast. (It is also frequently called Monte Carlo though, to be accurate, Monte Carlo is no more than a district of Monaco.) Monaco is a semi-independent state, synonymous the world over with chic, expensive luxury, and high glamor, bursting with fun for billionaires—and for lesser mortals, too. Every square inch of this tiny European state is built on or over, except for the Principality's luxuriant gardens, happily preserved regardless of their development potential.

● **Menton**
Menton is the last town on the Riviera before the Italian border, across which lies Ventimiglia where the Niçois and Mentonnais go to buy their hard liquor (it's cheaper). There's no great luxury in Menton, but you will find numerous good, medium-priced hotels here, in the warmest part of the Riviera. Menton is a quiet, respectable town, steadily growing livelier as it tries to shake off its traditional image as a place where senior citizens spend their last few gentle years, and to provide its neighbors to the west with some competition in the hedonism stakes.

SEAFOOD SUPREME

One of the chief delights of a vacation in France is the opportunity it gives to get to know the cooking of a particular region and to make friends with the local wines. The Riviera is not in quite the same culinary league as the rest of the country, even though some of the most prestigious restaurants—garlanded with nosegays of Michelin rosettes—are located here. The swarms of tourists who flood the coast at the height of the season have ensured that there are plenty of fast food outlets around, but there are also hundreds of thoroughly respectable eateries. As always, the clue to finding somewhere that offers both good food *and* good value is to keep your eyes skinned for the places which are patronized by a high proportion of Frenchmen. If, for example, you are wandering around Nice looking for lunch, you might spot the fact that the local office workers cross the promenade des Anglais to settle down to a superb meal on the beach at Ruhl Plage.

Local specialties on the Riviera mean, first and foremost, seafood. Not to be missed is *bouillabaisse*, the famous fish stew. In its classic form it consists of four or five kinds of fish: the villainous-looking *rascasse* (red scorpion fish), *grondin* (sea robin), *baudroie* (goose fish), *congre* (conger eel), and *rouget* (mullet). The whole lot is simmered in a stock of onions, tomatoes, garlic, olive oil, and saffron, which gives the dish its golden color. Other fish and shellfish—crab and crayfish—are often added, especially in classier establishments, to justify a phenomenal price. When presented properly, the broth is served first, with *croutons* and *rouille*, a creamy garlic sauce that you spoon in to suit your taste. The fish comes separately, and the ritual is to put pieces into the broth after having a go at the soup on its own. *Bouillabaisse* originated as a dish which fishermen cooked for themselves using fish they were unable to sell. Today, at its best, it's an expensive luxury. But, expensive though it is, beware of restaurants offering *bouillabaisse* for less than 150 frs. per person; it's unlikely to be authentic. A good sign, however, is when you have to order it a day in advance.

The most distinctive food on the Riviera comes from Nice. It's a curious mixture of Parisian, Provençale and Italian cuisine, pungent with garlic, olives, anchovies, and steaming shellfish. Among the specialties here are: *pissaladière*, an onion tart laced with black olive purée and anchovies; *pan bagnat*, a French loaf—a *baguette*—split down the middle, soaked in olive oil and garnished with tomatoes, radishes, peppers, onion, hard boiled eggs, black olives, and a sprig of basil; *l'estocaficada*, a ragout of stockfish (air-dried unsalted fish—often cod) soaked in water before cooking and served with potatoes, tomatoes, peppers, and courgettes (squash); and *socca*, an enormous pancake made from chick-pea flour and olive oil, and baked in an oven like pizza or sometimes fried in oil. When cooked it is sliced into finger-lickin' portions with an oyster knife. It's eaten in the bars of the old town and port and washed down with a thick red wine or a little glass of *pointu*, chilled rosé.

Provence is not one of France's great wine regions, but there are plenty of good wines to enjoy. Try the white wines from Cassis and the whites and reds from Bandol. In addition, Nice has the distinction of being the only major city in France other than Bordeaux which produces its own *appellation contrôlée* wines within the city limits. These are the excellent Bellet reds, whites, and rosés. Be sure to sample them when you're here.

Riviera Briefing

Make the French National Tourist Office the first stop when you start to plan your visit to the Riviera. There are offices around the globe which can supply a wealth of information, much of it free and all of it useful. The principal English-speaking offices are:

- **In the U.S.:** 610 Fifth Avenue, New York, NY 10020 (212-757-1125); 645 North Michigan Avenue, Chicago, IL 60611 (312-337-6301); 103 World Trade Center, Dallas, TX 75258 (214-742-7011); 9401 Wilshire Boulevard, Suite 314, Beverly Hills, CA 90212 (213-272-2661).
- **In Canada:** 1981 Avenue McGill College, Montréal, Québec H3A 2W9 (514-931-3855); 1 Dundas Street West, Suite 2405, Box 8, Toronto, Ontario M5G 1Z3 (416-593-4717).
- **In the U.K.:** 178 Piccadilly, London W1V OAL (01-491 7622).

The help of the local tourist offices is an almost indispensable complement to any guidebook. It is well worth while calling at the local office soon after arriving anywhere: the relevant addresses are given in each chapter.

The office may be called **Maison du Tourisme, Office de Tourisme,** or **Syndicat d'Initiative,** but each will display the international "i" sign, meaning "information."

The English-speaking staff will usually be able to give you a good town plan and complete lists of hotels and furnished apartments to investigate, of car rental firms, of specialist shops, of doctors, museums, and art galleries, as well as details of excursions by bus, train, and boat, and of places where sports equipment can be hired. Most important of all, they can give you lists of forthcoming events—festivals, concerts, and races. Many offices can book you into hotels. Offices in Cannes and Nice are also **Accueil de France** members (literally "French Welcome"), meaning that they can book hotel rooms for you anywhere in France for the cost of a telex, up to eight days in advance. You must pay a deposit, but the sum will be deducted from the hotel bill.

There are two points to remember when dealing with local tourist offices: the staff is strictly forbidden to make value judgments on hotels or restaurants, that is the realm of the guidebook; on the other hand, they are able to provide you with up-to-the-minute details on events, closed museums, road conditions, and the hundred and one other little bits of local knowledge that naturally lie outside the scope of an annually published book.

Prices

Riviera prices are about the same as Paris prices—you are encouraged to spend money here. However it is possible to find small, inexpensive hotels—especially in Nice—and those on a low budget should either look out for hotels whose rooms have kitchenettes, encouraging self-catering, or should perhaps consider camping. Be warned, though, that campsites along the coast become impossibly crowded in the summer, and finding a place at the last minute can be very difficult.

The great palace hotels of the Riviera have a style

and gloss that is unlike anything to be found anywhere else, and even if you can't stay in them, you should feel free to visit. A cup of coffee at the exclusive Negresco in Nice may cost three times what you would pay in an ordinary café, but it's a bargain entrance fee for a stroll around the amazing public rooms. Besides having one of France's best (and most expensive) restaurants, even the Negresco has a moderately priced eatery, and many other palace hotels can offer a similar range.

- **Money Matters.** Safeguard yourself by taking traveler's checks, and noting the serial numbers separately; but get some francs, too, before you leave home. The airport banks will be open whenever you arrive, but lines are often long, and rates are poor.

Banks are open from 9 to 4, Monday to Friday, though some close from 12 to 2:30. They all close the day before a public holiday. You can change money at hotels, some stores, and even the odd restaurant, but you'll invariably get the best rate at a bank.

The major credit cards are accepted at most of the better hotels, restaurants, and shops, but check the doors and windows for the usual stickers; there are still some Riviera proprietors who refuse to accept *any* cards—with a truly thrifty outlook, they don't see why they should be paying over their hard earned francs as a percentage to a credit card firm, just for someone else's convenience.

CLIMATE

The mild and balmy Riviera climate is legendary (especially among the British, who don't have a climate, only weather).

The novelist Tobias Smollett was a bad-tempered English grumbler, but an accurate observer. He was at Nice (for his health) in January 1764, long before the place attracted visitors. He stayed for over a year, and his notes can hardly be bettered.

> When I stand upon the rampart, and look around me, I can

scarce help thinking myself enchanted ... The plain presents nothing but gardens, full of green trees, loaded with oranges, lemons, citrons, and bergamots, which make a delightful appearance. ... Such is the serenity of the air, that you see nothing above your head for several months together, but a charming blue expanse, without cloud or speck. Whatever clouds may be formed by evaporation from the sea, they seldom or never hover over this small territory; but, in all probability, are attracted by the mountains that surround it, and there fall in rain or snow ... This air being dry, pure, heavy, and elastic, must be agreeable to the constitution of those who labor under disorders arising from weak nerves, obstructed perspiration, relaxed fibres, a viscidity of lymph, and a languid circulation ... [Smollett was a doctor].

In summer, the air is cooled by a regular sea-breeze blowing from the east ... It dies away about six or seven; and immediately after sunset, is succeeded by an agreeable land-breeze from the mountains ... About the winter solstice [21 December] the people of Nice expect wind and rain, which generally lasts, with intervals, till the beginning of February: but even during this, their worst weather, the sun breaks out occasionally, and you may take the air either a-foot or on horseback every day; for the moisture is immediately absorbed by the earth ... They likewise lay their account with being visited with showers of rain and gusts of wind in April ... A week's rain in the middle of August makes them happy ... but the rainy season is about the autumnal equinox, or rather something later ...

I have described the agreeable side of this climate; and now I will point out its inconveniences. In the winter, but especially in the spring, the sun is so hot, that one can hardly take any exercise ... without being thrown into a sweat; and the wind at this season is so cold and piercing, that it often produces a mischievous effect on the pores thus opened. If the heat rarefies the blood and juices, while the cold air constringes the fibres ... inflammatory disorders must ensue ... During the heats of summer, some few persons of gross habits have, in consequence of violent exercise and excess, been seized with putrid fevers ... [you have been warned] but the people in general are healthy, even those that take very little exercise: a strong presumption in favour of the climate.

Here are some figures for Antibes, to show the typical four seasons of the year on the Riviera:

- **January**—Average daily maximum temperature 54° F/12° C (record 66° F/19° C)

    Average daily minimum temperature 43° F/6° C (record 28° F/-2° C)

    Average number of days with some rain 8

    Average number of days with some frost 1

    Average number of days with some fog or snow 0
- **April**—Average daily maximum temperature 63° F/17° C (record 81° F/27° C)

    Average daily minimum temperature 50° F/10° C (record 37° F/3° C)

    Average number of days with some rain 7

    Average number of days with some frost, fog or snow 0
- **July**—Average daily maximum temperature 82° F/28° C (record 95° F/35° C)

    Average daily minimum temperature 66° F/19° C (record 52° F/11° C)

    Average number of days with some rain 1

    Average number of days with some frost, fog or snow 0
- **October**—Average daily maximum temperature 68° F/20° C (record 81° F/27° C)

    Average daily minimum temperature 55° F/13° C (record 41° F/5° C)

    Average number of days with some rain 9

    Average number of days with some frost, fog or snow 0

Move inland, away from the Riviera, and the climate is different. Tende is 27 miles from the coast, 2,100 feet up; it has 20 days of frost in January. Move west from the Riviera and you meet the windchill factor: the dreaded Mistral blows through Avignon on 100 days a year, while the Riviera nestles below its protective mountains.

Paris has about 24 inches of rain a year, falling on 160 days. The Riviera has about 27 inches, but it falls on only 80 days. Paris gets about 1,810 hours of sunshine a year, London 1,500—the Riviera gets over 2,800.

In winter there can be a disagreeably damp southeast wind. In July and August the usual sparkling clarity of the air can be veiled by evaporation from the sea; but seabreezes prevent the coast from growing as hot as the interior, unless the Sirocco blows from Africa. In fall there are often a few thunderstorms.

One side effect of sunny days and infrequent rain is that forests become dry and fires are a major hazard. You are not supposed even to smoke in the forests, let alone to light picnic barbecues, yet people do these things, and in 1986 hundreds of acres were burnt around Eze and the village was only just saved.

All in all, the Riviera climate is fairly reliable. It keeps close, month by month and year by year, to the projected figures.

Time zones

France is six hours ahead of Eastern Standard Time and one hour ahead of Greenwich Mean Time. The French put their clocks forward an hour in the spring and back an hour in the fall, at more or less the same time as the clocks are changed in the U.S. and Britain, so the time difference remains constant.

Entry and customs

Nationals from other EEC countries need only a valid passport; other foreign nationals—e.g. U.S. citizens—need a visa as well. Contact your travel agent or the French Government Tourist Office for details on obtaining a visa, which you must get before you leave home. Allow time for some delay, and expect to pay a small fee.

There are two levels of duty-free allowance for travelers entering France: one, for those coming from an EEC country; two, for those coming from any other country.

● In the first category you may import duty free: 300 cigarettes, or 150 cigarillos, or 75 cigars, or 400 gr. of

RIVIERA BRIEFING

tobacco. You can also import five liters of wine, one and a half liters of alcohol over 22° proof, or three liters of alcohol less than 22° proof; plus, 75 gr. of perfume and three-eighths of a liter of toilet water; plus, for those over 15, other goods to the value of 2,000 frs. (400 frs. for those under 15).

• In the second category you may import duty free: 200 cigarettes, or 100 cigarillos, or 50 cigars, or 250 gr. of tobacco (these allowances are doubled if you live outside Europe); plus, two liters of wine or one liter of alcohol more than 22° proof; plus, 50 gr. of perfume and a quarter of a liter of toilet water; plus, for those over 15, other goods to the value of 300 frs. (150 frs. for those under 15).

Any amount of French currency can be imported into France. Foreign currencies converted into francs may be reconverted into foreign currency up to the equivalent of 5,000 frs. Similarly, no more than 5,000 frs. may be exported. No more than the equivalent of 2,000 frs. in foreign currency may be exported.

Getting there and around

• **By Air.** The Riviera is easy to get to, and easy to get around. Nice airport handles over four million passengers a year, and services the whole coast. There are seven flights a week from New York, about 20 from London, over 100 from Paris, and you can fly there direct from another 76 cities in 31 countries. A fairly comprehensive system of buses, minibuses, and railroad links ferry passengers to other Riviera centers—Antibes, Juan-les-Pins, Villeneuve, Cannes, Monaco, Menton, and Vence are all covered.

• **By Train.** It is almost as easy to get to the Riviera by train from Paris as it is by air. Mainline expresses whizz down from the French capital, stopping at Toulon, St.-Raphael, Cannes, Antibes, and Nice. The trip from Paris to Nice takes about seven hours. There are also express trains from Italy and from Spain. Those who want to arrive fresh can put their car on the overnight train in Paris and wake up in Nice, using the Motorail (*Train Auto-Couchette*) service.

The train is a practical and inexpensive way of getting around the Riviera. The railroad is squeezed between the beach, the coast road, and the buildings. It burrows through the cliffs and sweeps past the bays, offering spectacular views. In fact, you can use the local trains just as if they were buses. They stop at dozens of little stations, attractively spruce with wrought-iron canopies and tubs of flowers—some of them seem hardly to have changed since the days of the Blue Train. The stations have the advantage, too, of being mostly in the middle of towns, meaning that you never have far to walk. Cannes rail station, for instance, is only five minutes from the luxury hotels and the beaches of La Croisette.

To find train stations look for the sign **Gare SNCF,** and once you've got your ticket, remember to punch it in the machine before going onto the platform, otherwise you'll be fined. Taxis are available at most stations.

For more train information, call: Nice 93–87–50–50; Cannes 93–99–50–50; Monte Carlo 93–30–25–53.

● **By Bus.** Like the trains, local buses cover a network of routes along the Riviera, but go to many out-of-the-way places that can't be reached by train. Timetables are available from tourist offices, rail stations, and the local **Gare Routières** (bus depots).

● **By Car.** All roads, even secondary ones, are well maintained and signed, but beware of the maniacal French drivers who use them! You'll find that cars pass at speed on either the left or the right—it's a giant slalom at times—so drive defensively. The French express themselves extravagantly with horns and abuse, and have an explicit repertoire of semaphore. Don't take it seriously.

The corniche roads along the coast here are some of the most famous in the world. For raw drama of mountains and sea, take one of the corniches that run between Nice and Menton. But they are not for those in a hurry—for the visitor who needs to get quickly from one place to another there is the A8 autoroute, which bypasses Aix, just above Marseille, travels eastwards to reach the coast near Fréjus. It also serves Cannes and Nice, tunnels through the hills above Monaco, and passes Menton to reach Italy just before Ventimiglia. While hardly touristic, the autoroute has a manmade splendor, with magnificent views almost all the way along.

Apart from the autoroute, the going on Riviera coastal roads is slow, with frequent traffic jams. On the other hand, inland driving is a delight, opening up some fascinating places that are hard to reach without a car. One of the chief snags is that parking can be difficult and expensive.

Hotels and restaurants

This book offers a selection of hotels in the main centers. Each chapter has detailed descriptions of one or two hotels that have caught our attention by offering something special; these are usually, though not always, among the more expensive. Other hotels are described more briefly. Its long decades as a tourist mecca have ensured that the Riviera is very well supplied with hotels in every grade. Tourist offices will have full lists and details.

If your budget is tight, consider the option of staying somewhere inexpensive for most of the holiday, and then booking in at a top hotel for one night, to sample the luxurious lifestyle that the Riviera caters to so well.

When it comes to restaurants, we also aim to discuss a representative selection, including some of the world famous temples of gastronomy. But if the menu outside a restaurant not listed here attracts you, and the place seems reasonably full of happy-looking people, don't be discouraged by our silence.

● **Hotel Prices.** We have divided all the hotels in our lists into four grades, each determined solely by price. They are (L) Luxury; (E) Expensive; (M) Moderate; and (I) Inexpensive.

In 1987 you could figure on paying, for two people in a double room:

Luxury (L)	1,000 frs. and up
Expensive (E)	500 frs. and up
Moderate (M)	250 to 500 frs.
Inexpensive (I)	120 to 250 frs.

These are high season prices. In some (L) and (E) hotels low-season prices can be much less. As an extreme example, the same room at Loews in La Napoule was 608 frs. from November to the end of March; 1,542 frs. in July and August and during the Cannes film festival; and 1,305 frs. the rest of the year.

Breakfast is often an extra, 20 to 90 frs. per person. You may, of course, find it more fun to have breakfast in a café, in which case you can expect to pay about 20 frs.

● **Restaurant Prices.** We have divided all the restaurants into three grades, each determined solely by price. They are (E) Expensive; (M) Moderate; and (I) Inexpensive.

In 1987 a three-course meal, with a half bottle of wine, or a carafe of house wine, for one person, cost:

Expensive (E)	300 frs. and up
Moderate (M)	150 to 300 frs.
Inexpensive (I)	150 frs. and below

In the most celebrated of the gourmet shrines the prices will be well up on the 300 frs. And bear in mind that there are overlaps: an Inexpensive restaurant may well offer temptations in the Moderate or even the Expensive categories. One of the secrets to eating well for less—or even eating superbly for less—is to take advantage of the set menus that almost all restaurants offer. By the way, a menu in French is *la carte,* while a set menu is *le menu.* Many famous places offer a "tasting" set menu—*menu dégustation*—which includes small portions of their most celebrated dishes, giving you the chance of experiencing the chefs' expertise without breaking the bank.

Tipping

Hotels, restaurants, and cafés will always include the service charge on the check, so don't tip unless you think it's really justified—around 12 to 15 percent is usual for special service. Otherwise, tip as you would back home.

Shopping

The whole of the Riviera offers incredible shopping opportunities, if your bank balance can stand it! All the major tourist towns have a veritable glut of chic shops of every kind; indeed, a recent statistic has revealed that Cannes, with a permanent population of around 72,000, has more than 2,500 shops. The same kind of story goes for Nice, Menton, Monte Carlo, St.-Tropez, and so on. But this doesn't mean that the Côte d'Azur is a kind of translated Fifth Avenue; there are still good traditional crafts to be found, especially if you venture away from the coast into the mountains. Olivewood articles, ceramics, dried flowers, and perfumes are all age-old products here.

Even in the towns there are bargains and hidden specialties to be found. For local color, make for the street markets, ablaze with flowers, and piled high with fruits, vegetables, and cheeses of all kinds.

Tax refunds

Visitors to France (i.e. normally resident outside the country) may be given the opportunity to save money by being exonerated from part of the value-added tax (VAT in French) on certain goods. Discounts obtained in this way range from 13 percent to 23 percent (on "luxury" goods such as jewelry or perfumes). You should be aware that shopkeepers are not legally obliged to offer this discount, so you can't insist on getting it. You will find that department stores are the best places for you to benefit from the system, as most of them employ a special staff to operate it, as do other shops that have a large foreign clientele. Small boutiques are emphatically not equipped to deal efficiently with the complicated paperwork—in France *all* state paperwork is complicated—and the system is liable to break down.

This is how it works. For a start, the total value of your purchases in a single store must be at least 800 frs. if you live outside the EEC; if you live in an EEC member state discounts are obtainable only on *single items* costing at least 1,030 frs. Some stores will simply state a price after deduction of the discount. But they'll be taking a risk, because if you don't do your bit by handing on the documentation to the customs, they'll be out of pocket. The great majority will ask you to pay the full amount and the discount will be sent to you in due course. The store will fill out a form in quadruplicate, giving you three copies and keeping one. Make sure that if you live outside the EEC they haven't filled in an EEC form by mistake and vice versa. You must give details of your bank account, or that of friends in France—reimbursements cannot be made to private addresses. If you live outside the EEC you present two of the forms to the customs official on leaving the country—he will probably ask to see the goods in question to make sure that you haven't just been doing a favor to a French friend! Make sure to leave plenty of time for this operation. If you live in an EEC country, the papers are dealt with by the customs official when you reach your own country.

Frankly, you may well think it's not worth the time and trouble, unless you're making really big purchases. And EEC residents in particular should bear in mind that the customs official you present your forms to back home may decide to charge you customs duty on the goods—which will easily cancel out the VAT refund.

St.-Tropez

St.-Tropez—so they say—is synonymous with sun, sea, celebrities and sex; a place that is famous for being famous; but it wasn't always so.

St.-Tropez was essentially an exceptionally pretty port and fishing village which, even now that it has become one of the best known of the Mediterranean resorts, remains quite small, with only some 6,000 permanent inhabitants. It stands at the southern end of a beautiful bay—but otherwise doesn't give the impression of being particularly well placed. It is out on a limb, on the end of a peninsula, scorned by the railway which passes by on the other side of the Massif des Maures, and a prey to the northwesterly Mistral and to chill, wet, easterly winds which empty it in winter to such an extent that few, if any, hotels and restaurants stay open between November and March.

The town is said to be named after St.-Torpo or Torpetius, who was martyred for his faith by Nero. He was beheaded and his corpse and head were put into a boat on the Italian coast, together with a dog and a rooster, and pushed out to sea. The saint's companions piously refrained from eating his remains, and the boat with its curious crew docked safely in the harbor here.

St.-Tropez has been "discovered" several times. The painter Paul Signac fell in love with it in 1892 and settled here. Other painters followed for lengthy working visits—Bonnard, Camoin, Matisse, and Segonzac. Between the wars Colette succumbed to its charm, as had Guy de Maupassant many years earlier. Then in the mid-1950s Roger Vadim made *And God Created Woman* here, starring the young Brigitte Bardot, and from that time on St.-Tropez has attracted stars, the beautiful people, the rich, the raunchy, and the extravagantly eccentric.

Some of the famous actually live here. Brigitte Bardot, who nowadays gives all her energies to the protection and support of animals, has a house in St.-Tropez. Others arrive from elsewhere in open-topped Jaguars and Porsches—Rolls Royces are more at home in Cannes. Some glide up in yachts and moor in the harbor, sipping evening drinks on the decks in full view of the café terraces around the port.

The place is intensely crowded in summer, but the atmosphere is as tolerant as it is glitzy. There is a sizable gay community, with many allied bars, beaches, and nightclubs to frequent. St.-Tropez is a place where you can wear what you like, and go to bed at dawn, but most of all it is a place to see and be seen. Celebrity-spotting is the foremost local sport, and largely free—unless your quarry can only be found deep in an expensive restaurant.

It is a fine resort for an extended stay, especially if you are young, rich, and chic, but even a one-night visit is worthwhile, particularly if you can stay at the Byblos. Or just come to drink coffee on the port, ramble round the Old Town, and pick up a little of the gloss of it all before moving on.

Exploring

A good place to start out is at the "new harbor," the *nouveau bassin*, for private pleasure boats, because there's a large parking lot here, and also the bus station. With the sea on your left, walk around to the "old harbor," enjoying the life of the port and the views across the bay as you go.

Just inland from the southwest corner of the port stands the **Musée de l'Annonciade.** This was a chapel which has been sensitively converted into an art gallery to house the personal collection of a local resident, Georges Grammont, who bequeathed it to the town. A few sculptures and a hundred paintings (mainly neo-Impressionist) are displayed here, so that the visitor can glimpse St.-Tropez through the eyes of Signac and other outstanding artists from the turn of the century. Open 10 to 12, 3 to 7, June to September; 10 to 12, 2 to 6, October and December to May; closed November and Tuesdays. (Tel. 94–97–04–01.)

Next, make for the **Sénéquier,** the café with the big terrace right on the port. In many ways this is the heart of St.-Tropez; it provides a front row seat from which to observe the multicolored scene—and its aperitifs, coffees, and ice creams are not much more expensive than those served in cafés of lesser renown. Arrive at breakfast time and you will find those who have danced all night mingling with those who have just got up; arrive at sunset, and the glory of the view may distract you from people-watching.

Almost next door is **Le Gorille,** another café with its own devoted following. It took its name from its exceptionally hirsute manager—but, alas, he died in 1986, and though the name lingers on, his successors tend to be smooth men.

Continue in the same direction around the busy harbor, where fishing boats and luxury yachts, tour boats and a few commercial craft all lilt around on the water together. If the wind isn't too strong, walk out along the mole, the harbor wall, for a good view of Ste.-Maxime across the sparkling bay, of the hills of Estérel and, on a clear day, of the distant Alps.

Retrace your steps along the mole and the quayside to the tourist office near the Café Sénéquier, and then take the rue de la Citadelle which leads away from the port up to the **Citadel** itself. This is a forbidding hexagonal fortress, with three round tiled towers, which dates from the 16th century. The view from up here is even more extensive than it is from the end of the mole.

The Citadel keep houses the **Musée de la Maritime,** which is an out-station of the Chaillot Palace Museum in Paris. This annex is a modest museum, devoted to boats, with some detailed models of ships, old and new. There are also paintings and engravings which illustrate the history of St.-Tropez with particular reference to its relations with the sea, and even a cut-in-half torpedo (the French Navy makes them near here). Open 10 to 12, 3 to 7, June to September; 10 to 12, 2 to 4, October and December to May; closed Tuesdays and November.

Leaving the Citadel, make your way down to the Montée Ringrave and so to the **place des Lices,** also called the place Carnot (the French habit of varying the names of streets and squares can be confusing). This is where the market is held on Tuesdays and Saturdays, and where *pétanque*—a southern version of *boules* using steel balls—is played. Pétanque players and film stars take refreshment at the **Café des Arts**—why not go with the flow and join them?

Take the rue Sibilli, which leaves the place Carnot from the northwest, and follow it back to the port. This is a street made for window shopping, lined as it is with chic boutiques, outposts of Paris, displaying slick little high fashion numbers to suit everyone—male, female, and all stages of unisex.

The one thing St.-Tropez can't offer is a good beach immediately in town. But there are fabulous beaches to be found along the route des Plages, in a three mile stretch which begins two and a half miles outside town, running south. If you don't have a car, and you must have a beach, there are four hire firms in town.

There are public beaches here, though much further

25 ST.-TROPEZ

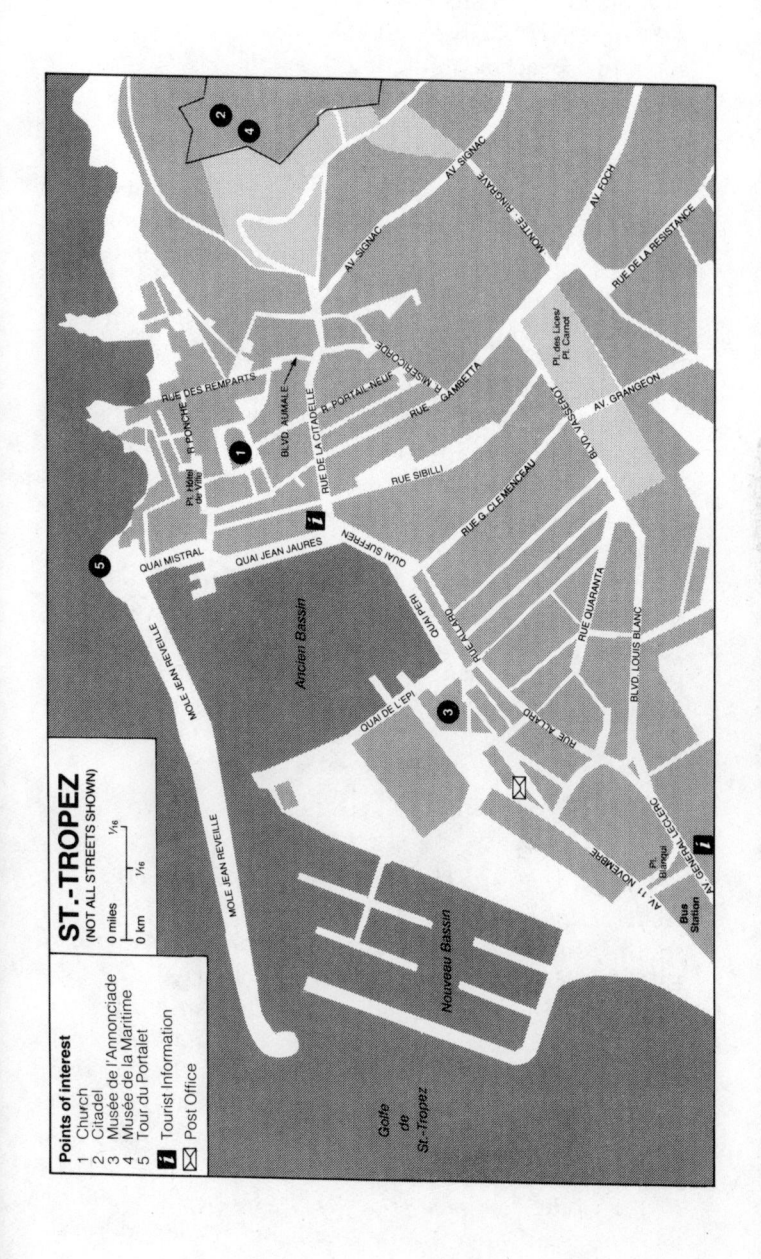

on, but it's best to go to the private ones, even though it means paying. **Tahiti Plage, Club 55,** and **Moorea** are fashionable, with Moorea in the lead, but there are many others. It is perfectly acceptable, of course, to go topless on all the beaches, though not compulsory; the **Blouch** is happy about total nudity; some are favored by gays. You won't need a diagram to tell you which is which. Many of the beaches serve lunches, mostly at (M) prices.

There is one spot near St.-Tropez (four miles west) that you shouldn't miss—**Port Grimaud,** an imitation Provençal fishing village, built in the early 1960s. Although it's a complete fake, it has been brilliantly designed with all the right local elements—little bridges over lazy canals, attractive small houses in a range of sun-drenched colors, alleyways, and a village square vibrant with flowers. You can't drive around, so park as you go in and explore on foot. Alternately, hire a drive-it-yourself motorboat and cruise the canals. There's a terrific view from the top of the church tower over the port, and across to St.-Tropez.

If you're there for lunch, try **La Tartane** (M), tel. 94-56-38-32; open from mid-March to end October; or **La Marina** (M), tel. 94-56-25-50, where you can enjoy Provençal dishes while you relax and watch the local residents—it's a fairly classy place—tending their yachts.

INFORMATION

- **Tourist Offices.** The main tourist office is at 23 av. Général Leclerc (tel. 94-97-41-41); it's a short walk south from the big parking lot by the sea. **American Express** is at the same address (tel. 94-97-20-66). There's another tourist office at quai Jean-Jaurès (tel. 94-97-45-21) near Café Sénéquier. Both are open April through September, Monday to Saturday 9 to 7 (to 8 from mid-June), Sunday and public holidays 10 to 1; October through March, Monday to Saturday 9 to 6:30; closed Sunday.
- **Post Code.** The post code for St.-Tropez is 83990. It must be used when writing to any St.-Tropez address.

- **Car Hire. Avis,** 13 blvd. Louis Blanc (tel. 94–97–03–10). **Europcar,** place de la Poste (tel. 94–97–15–41). **Hertz,** rue Nouvelle Poste (tel. 94–97–22–01). **Interent,** Station du Pilori (tel. 94–97–00–37).
- **Boat Hire. Performance Marine,** Baie des Canoubiers (tel. 94–54–84–11). **Sportmer,** 8 place Blanqui (tel. 94–97–23–33). Sale and rental. **Suncap Company,** Passage du Port (tel. 94–97–11–23). With or without crew.
- **Helicopter. Heli-Station,** (tel. 94–97–36–45). See also *Monaco* and *Nice* chapters.

ACCESS

St.-Tropez can be tricky to get to by public transport—as we have already mentioned it isn't on the railroad. Nor is a car ideal, because there are likely to be traffic jams en route, and parking problems once you arrive.

Those determined to come by car, and traveling from the west, should leave the A8 highway at Le Cannet-des-Maures and take D558 via La Garde-Freinet and Grimaud, 25 slow but scenic miles. Alternatively, stay on A8 for a further 12 miles, turning off at Le Muy and taking the 23 miles via Ste.-Maxime, a longer but potentially faster route.

The best and most enjoyable way to arrive is to use the ferry service from Ste.-Maxime to St.-Tropez across the bay. It runs six or seven boats a day out of season, and one every half hour or so in the high season. The boats don't take cars, but you won't need one in St.-Tropez, except perhaps to get to the beaches, and there are hire cars available for that.

In summer, there are also boat services linking St.-Raphael—which you *can* reach by rail—and St.-Tropez, but they are rather irregular. There are also eight buses a day running from St.-Raphael to St.-Tropez.

For a really dramatic entry, a helicopter can be chartered from Nice airport. In 1987 it cost 4,000 frs. to take four people.

HAPPENINGS

The two most important happenings are the *bravades,* or fiestas, which are very personal to the permanent inhabitants. The first, on May 16 and 17, celebrates St.-Tropez himself; the second, on June 15, falls on the anniversary of the defeat of 22 marauding Spanish galleys by the local militia, who sent them speedily on their way in 1637. Neither is put on for the tourists—both would continue if all visitors inexplicably left town—yet visitors are very welcome to watch the fun, which takes the form of processions, in costume, with supporting bands and musket shots.

There is a military parade on May 8, Victory Day; fireworks and dancing in the street on July 14, Bastille Day; and a Rolls Royce rally in September. Otherwise, there are concerts throughout the year (jazz, rock, orchestral, and chamber), cycle races, yacht races, a windsurfing race across the bay, and a golf competition. Dates and details are available from the tourist office.

But, in St.-Tropez, the most typical happenings are unscheduled, and depend on who's about and what the weather's like. With luck there's always something going on around the port, as you sip your aperitif on a café terrace, always someone well-known to see—or, at the very least, some vaguely familiar figure in dark glasses to speculate about.

LODGING

Byblos (L), av. Signac (tel. 94–97–00–04). 70 rooms, 37 suites. Open March through October. The Byblos is unique. There are other expensive palace hotels up and down the Riviera with a similarly magnificent standard of facilities, but the difference at the Byblos is that it is designed not to intimidate. There are no daunting corridors stretching as if to infinity here. Every room and suite has lavishly appointed bathrooms, 24-hour room service, air-conditioning, TV, private terrace, or balcony; and in the public areas there's a swimming pool, two restaurants, and two nightclubs, all open to nonresidents, and a solarium and Jacuzzi for residents only.

The hotel is a complex of over 100 rooms and suites, decorated with ingenuity, taste, and humor. It seems almost like a Provençal village, with its cottagey suites built round courtyards paved with Picasso-inspired tiles and fragrant with magnolias and orange trees. Each room is different, with cheerful, amusing touches, subtle lighting, and good pictures.

Ideally, visit in off-season so you can ask to see a series of rooms just for the pleasure of the tour. Prices are lower off-season, too, though still out of reach of most pockets. 1987 high season prices (May 27 to September 27, and the Easter and May 1 weekends) were 1,460 frs. for a double room and 2,290 frs. for a suite. Low season rates were 970–1,360 frs. for a room and from 1,620 frs. for a suite.

Of the two nightclubs, **Les Caves du Roy** is the best in St.-Tropez, while **Le Chabichou** is the town's best restaurant. Though in the hotel, they are technically independent; see below for further details. **La Braiserie** (M), the hotel's other restaurant, is by the pool. There's also a dimly lit disco, **Le Krak des Chevaliers,** or the **Eddie Barclay Room,** an imitation of an English billiards room, with leather armchairs and sporting prints. Truly, there's nowhere quite like the Byblos.

Résidence de la Pinede (L), plage de la Bouillabaisse (tel. 94–97–04–21). 40 rooms, 5 suites. Open mid-April through mid-October. This luxury hotel is a little under a mile out of town, right on the sea. It boasts its own beach, a pool, and a dining room whose glass walls can be folded away to take full advantage of Mediterranean weather. Eat in the shade of the pines, with the sea murmuring discreetly at your elbow. There are all the usual first-class facilities and, in expectation of wealthy customers, a safe is provided in every room.

Le Yaca (E), blvd. Aumale (tel. 94–97–11–79). 22 rooms. Open mid-April through mid-October. This is a delightful hotel, right in the center of town, made up of three village houses grouped around a swimming pool in a garden. It is beautifully decorated, and supplied with all the creature comforts you would expect of a luxury hotel. There's a good (M) restaurant, which opens for dinner only, but there are plenty of attractive places to eat lunch within a few minutes' stroll.

Ermitage (M), av. Signac (tel. 94-97-52-33). 29 rooms. Open mid-December through October. Possibly the ideal, moderately priced, town hotel, in a comfortable and elderly building, with genuine old-fashioned charm. Some of the rooms have a view of the bay and each has its own bathroom. There's no swimming pool, but the Byblos next door opens its pool to nonresidents. There's no restaurant, either, but there are numerous restaurants nearby.

La Tartane (M), route des Salins (tel. 94-97-58-16). 12 rooms. Open end March through early November. A group of attractively furnished, air-conditioned bungalows, stands around a pool. Breakfast is served on the individual terraces, and lunch by the pool, but you'll have to go elsewhere for dinner. Because La Tartane is small and two miles out of town, it is peaceful and free of crowds—but you do need a car to get out to it.

Les Lauriers (I), rue du Temple (tel. 94-97-04-88). 18 rooms. Open Easter through September. One of St.-Tropez's better inexpensive hotels. Les Lauriers doesn't have any of the frills—no air-conditioning, no pool, no minibar in the room—but it's comfortable value for money.

Les Palmiers (I), 26 blvd. Vasserot (tel. 94-97-01-61). Open all year. Conveniently situated, right on the place des Lices, and with a little garden, too, this one is a bit more expensive than Les Lauriers, but not bad for high-lifers on a budget.

DINING

Le Chabichou (E), Hotel Byblos (tel. 94-54-80-00). Beautiful decor, impeccable service, superb food; a top restaurant *à la Riviera*. Chef Rochedy is famous for his delicate, inventive dishes, suitable for summer evenings —even his grilled fresh sardines win gourmets' praise. Foie gras and lobster are, as you might expect, on offer, but the adventurous can try creations like *daube de supions aux pieds de porc et févettes,* a stew of baby squid with pigs' feet and broad beans. It sounds disgusting in English but the flavor is delicious. There are some rare and special wines in the cellar, but if you've only got one fortune to spend it should go on the food—so try the eminently drinkable local wines.

Other Restaurants. There is no shortage of good eateries in St.-Tropez. Four medium-priced restaurants of a good standard spring to mind. There's the **Bistrot de la Marine** on the port (tel. 94–97–04–07), and the **Bistrot des Lices** (tel. 94–97–29–00), on the square of that name, is the haunt of show business types and has a barman renowned for his cocktails in a town where they are a way of life. Back on the port, look for **Le Girelier** (tel. 94–97–03–87), and **Leï Mouscardin** (tel. 94–97–01–53), which is sited at one end of the harbor, near the Tour du Portalet, and with sea views to eat by.

Highly recommended at the upper end of the inexpensive range is **l'Echalote,** 35 rue Allard (tel. 94–54–83–26), with a relaxing terrace, and very popular, excellent food, but don't be put off by the rather depressing exterior. **Lou Revelen,** 4 rue des Remparts (tel. 94–97–06–34), has a very acceptable Italian-influenced menu, plus regional dishes such as stuffed sardines.

NIGHTCLUBS

Les Caves du Roy, at the Byblos, is very much the "in" place; the decor might be thought stunningly vulgar, but the clientele is *tres* chic. Not everybody gets in; it's big, but often full, and it's as well to look as cool and stylish as you can to be sure of getting past the doorman.

New Jimmy's is the other top night spot, where Régine competes with Jacqueline Vessières who runs Les Caves du Roy. It's at the Résidence du Nouveau Port.

Next door to it is **Le Bal,** a gay hangout. **L'Esquinade,** in the rue du Four (the old part of the town), is where boy meets girl when dawn is breaking, and where thoughts of going to bed have little to do with sleep.

Shopping

St.-Tropez has lots and lots of boutiques, most of which open only in the season (to make great loads of hay while the sun shines). It's hard to recommend specific shops because they open and close down again with alarming rapidity. Wander round and see what's there—window shopping is a traditional St.-Tropez sport. More seriously, there are excellent handmade chocolates at **Georget,** in the rue Allard.

Excursions

Les iles d'Hyères

This trio of islands is sometimes called **Les Iles d'Or,** the golden isles, perhaps because of the coloring taken on by their rocks in certain lights.

The largest of the three, **Ile de Porquerolles,** is about five miles long by one mile wide; it's an idyllic place with heavy growths of myrtle, eucalyptus and pines, brilliant flowers, and rich vineyards. Film-makers come here when they need a stand-in for an unspoiled tropical location—and, happily, the protection of the state ensures that it will remain unspoiled.

There is a small village, and a few hotels and restaurants have been built discreetly around it, but the main attraction is the opportunity for taking enchanted walks, away from noise and traffic, with the scents from the luxuriant vegetation mingling with the tang of the surrounding sea. The best walk is from the little port across the island to the lighthouse, (*le phare*), a place of stupendous views. The round trip takes about one and a half hours. Or simply head eastwards, along the beaches, for as long as time or energy will allow.

The **Ile de Port-Cros** is smaller, three miles by one mile, and some say it would stand comparison with the Garden of Eden. It is a National Park and nature reserve which means that visitors have to behave themselves—no shooting, no camping, no underwater fishing, no fires, and no smoking, as forest fires are the bane of the Riviera. There are delightful paths, all clearly marked, the most magical of which is the two hour walk along the bosky Solitude Valley, starting at the charming little hotel **Le Manoir d'Hélène,** and returning along the route des Crâtes within sight of the sea.

The **Ile du Levant,** which is five miles long but only 1,300 yards wide, is less interesting. It is rocky, with great battlement-like cliffs, and much of it is owned by the French Navy—except for the village of **Heliopolis** which is a large nudist camp.

Getting There. There are various boat trips to the islands. The shortest crossing, from La Tour Fondue (at the end of the Giens peninsula near Hyères) to Ile de Porquerolles, takes 20 minutes and boats go half-hourly in season and two or three times a day the rest of the year.

From Hyères-Plage, at the mainland end of the peninsula, there are round-trip crossings to Port-Cros and Levant that take about an hour and a half. Boats make one to four trips daily from April through September, and one every alternate day in winter.

From Le Lavandou infrequent boats take a half hour to reach Port-Cros and 50 minutes to Porquerolles; from Cavalaire-sur-Mer they take rather longer, an hour to Port-Cros and two to Porquerolles. There are also summer sailings to all the islands from St.-Tropez itself. Details of all boat trips can be obtained from the tourist office.

St.-Tropez to Mandelieu

St.-Tropez, for all its fame and glamor, is something of an outpost of the Riviera, technically not even part of the Côte d'Azur. Because of this, and because there are no major resorts between St.-Tropez and Mandelieu, we will deal with that lengthy coastal strip in short.

The coastal road between St.-Tropez and Mandelieu, the N98, is a masterpiece of 19th-century engineering, heavily used by 20th-century traffic. It passes a succession of bays and beaches, almost every one of which has sprouted a minor seaside resort with private villas, cafés, and even shacks selling hot dogs.

Ste.-Maxime and Fréjus

Ste.-Maxime, on the opposite side of the bay to St.-Tropez, is altogether quieter and more sedate than its celebrated neighbor. It has a good beach, hotels in most price ranges except the very highest, and well-appointed campsites. A series of minor resorts separate it from Fréjus, which was called Forum Julii—Julius Caesar's Forum—in Roman times. Roman remains can still be seen here, as well as the early Gothic cathedral, with its ancient baptistry dating back to the beginning of the 5th century. Both are fascinating.

St.-Raphael merges with the eastern half of Fréjus—in fact now, the two are really one and the same town, with St.-Raphael forming the least interesting half—though it does have a number of reasonably priced hotels.

For a really good hotel, strike inland for three miles to the **Maphotel Golf de Valescure** (E), tel. 94–82–40–31. 40 rooms. Open March through September, and at Christmas and New Year. It has a restaurant for seafood and Provençale specialties, a garden with a pool and tennis courts, and, of course, golf. It's fairly high up, and attractively surrounded by pinetrees.

Massif de l'Estérel

The **Massif de l'Estérel,** a ruggedly wild and beautiful range of hills, lies between Fréjus-St.-Raphael and Mandelieu. Dedicated ramblers, who take to the hills in stout shoes, find a dramatic landscape of ragged, volcanic rocks, deep ravines, and dense scrub. Drivers can bypass it by taking the A8 expressway. An alternative is to drive along its northern flank on the tortuous N7, originally a Roman road, part of the Rome–Arles highway. Too busy to be much fun until the A8 drew away much of the traffic, the N7 is now an attractive road to travel along.

If you do take the N7, look out for an intersection called the Carrefour du Testannier, six miles from Fréjus. Turn right and follow the signs to **Forêt Domaniale de l'Estérel** and **Mont Vinaigre.** Here the reasonably hardy can leave their cars and take the 15-minute walk to the top of Mont Vinaigre where they will be rewarded by a magnificent view over the hills.

Agay

If you don't choose to take the inland route you can continue along the coast road which will bring you to the little resort of **Agay,** whose deep bay was once much favored by ancient Greek traders. Agay is a good base for the adventurous who want to explore the wild, romantic Estérel. It has a very good hotel: **Sol e Mar** (M), Le Dramont (tel. 94–95–25–60). 40 rooms. Open mid-April through mid-October. Its restaurant has a wonderful view, and the amenities include both a pool and a private beach.

Between here and Mandelieu there are more resorts, cafés, restaurants, and hotels scattered along the coast—look out especially for the excellent **Hôtel St.-Chris-**

tophe (E), tel. 93–75–41–36, in Miramar. 40 rooms. Open mid-March through mid-October. It has a lovely garden and, of course, swimming.

Mandelieu-La Napoule

Mandelieu and La Napoule were once two separate villages. Mandelieu is at the edge of the great mimosa plantations of La Croix des Gardes and the Tanneron Hills, while La Napoule lies just below it, on the coast. Nowadays they have merged together into one town, just five miles west of Cannes, which is being vigorously developed as an outdoor sports and amusement center.

The two golf courses—one eighteen hole and the other nine hole—were laid out long ago, but the lavish facilities for all kinds of water sports are more recent. You can sail, waterski, jetski, windsurf, go deep sea diving, or, for something a little less energetic, go fishing. There are several tennis courts right in town, a riding school just outside it, occasional polo games, and a chance to try parachuting. There is also one of France's top 20 restaurants, a luxury hotel with its own casino, several good, moderately priced hotels, and attractive campsites. Altogether it's an excellent place for a vacation of sporty days in the open air, self-indulgent evenings, and easy trips to Cannes.

Exploring

People come to Mandelieu-La Napoule to enjoy the sporting facilities—there are some excellent stretches of sandy beach between here and Cannes. It is not much of a place for sightseeing, though there is one prominent sight, the castle, down on the seafront, built onto part of a 14th-century fort, and which now houses the **Foundation Henry Clews.** By 1918 the structure was no more than a ruin. Then it was bought by an American sculptor, Henry Clews, and his architect wife, whose extensive rebuilding program resulted in the rather curious mixture of styles that can be seen today. The situation is attractive, the gardens are pleasant, and there are displays of some of the sculptor's works which it would be ungrateful to criticize. There are guided tours most afternoons and special exhibitions from time to time. The occasional use of the castle as a conference center causes it to be temporarily closed to the public, so don't plan a special visit without contacting the tourist office or phoning the foundation (tel. 93–49–95–05).

Information

- **Tourist Offices.** There are two tourist offices: at av. J. Aulas (tel. 93–49–95–31), near the rail station; and at av. de Cannes (tel. 93–49–14–39), near the highway exit for the town. Both are open seven days a week in high season, six days a week the rest of the year.
- **Post Code.** The postal code for Mandelieu-La Napoule is 06210, which must be used when writing to any Mandelieu-La Napoule address.
- **Car Hire. France Rent,** Mandelieu Garage, av. de Cannes (tel. 93–49–20–35), for bikes and mopeds, too. **Hertz,** Cannes-Mandelieu airport (tel. 93–48–00–63).

ACCESS

Although it is only five miles from Cannes, Mandelieu-La Napoule is hard to reach by public transport. It has a rail station and a few local trains which run here from Cannes —if you're coming from some other major center you'll need to change at Cannes. There is a bus connection with both Cannes and Nice. Coming from Nice airport, you'll need to get a bus to Cannes and then a local bus or train out. Taxis are available at Cannes, but this is a fairly expensive method of covering the ground.

Those with cars, however, will find the town conveniently situated because both the A8 expressway and the N7 coast road pass right through the center. The ideal solution for anyone without a car is to hire one in the town, or at the rail station in Nice or Cannes, or at Nice airport.

HAPPENINGS

Mandelieu-La Napoule is overwhelmed with fluffy golden flowers in February when *La Fête du Mimosa* welcomes the first blooming of these extraordinary plants which flourish in the Massif du Tanneron behind the town. Each year thousands of tons of mimosa are exported, and marching bands, elaborate flowery floats, and drum-majorettes take to the streets to celebrate the fact. What Mardi Gras is to Nice and the Lemon Fair is to Menton, the Mimosa Festival is to Mandelieu-La Napoule.

There are other fêtes in March, May, and July, and glittering firework shows in July and August, but it is the sporting events that are the most important. Throughout the season there are sailing regattas, windsurfing contests, golf championships, fishing competitions and, every August, the Kelly Challenge, a rowing regatta named after Grace Kelly's father who was a keen oarsman in his native Philadelphia. Full details of all these events are available from tourist offices.

Cannes's program of world famous events is readily accessible from Mandelieu-La Napoule.

LODGING

Loews (L), blvd. Henry Clews (tel. 93–49–90–00). 196 rooms, 30 suites. Open all year; November through March prices are reduced. With a mere 230 or so rooms, this is a smaller edition of the gargantuan Loew's at Monte Carlo: an ultra-modern, thoroughly glitzy, luxury hotel in a fine position beside the sea. All the rooms are air-conditioned and have balconies, and many of them overlook the Mediterranean. In addition, there's a swimming pool, shops, a bank, a travel agency, car hire, tennis courts—and 24-hour room service. The hotel's casino, bars, and two restaurants are all open to nonresidents. **La Brasserie** is in the (M) range, and the elegant **Chez Loulou** is (E), with excellent grilled fish.

Le Domaine d'Olival (E), 778 av. de la Mer (tel. 93–49–31–00). 18 suites. Closed November to mid-January. There are only 18 rooms and suites, so you'll be lucky to get in here in high season. All rooms are air-conditioned and have balconies or terraces, and each has been individually designed by the architect-owner. There's no hint of mass production. The hotel stands in its own beautifully cared-for gardens on the river—you can tie your boat up at its moorings—and there are tennis courts and a pool. Each room and suite has a little kitchen equipped to French standards, so you could turn out your own five-course gourmet meals should you feel like it. Some of the suites take six people, which brings the price per couple down to the (M) range, even in high season—especially if you go for one restaurant meal a day and self-catering for the rest of the time.

Ermitage du Riou (E), 3 blvd. du Bord de Mer (tel. 93–49–95–56). Closed November to mid-December. This is an excellent hotel, right on the port, with great views from many of the rooms, some of which have wide terraces. There's a pool, a garden, and air-conditioning in the restaurant, **Le Lamparo** (M), itself highly recommended for fine fish dishes.

Logis Sant Estello (I), Domaine de Barbossi, route de Fréjus (tel. 93–49–54–54). Open all year. This is a simple and charming place in the Domaine de Barbossi (see *Horse Riding* below). It's just a couple of miles inland and gives the impression of being right out in the country . . . except that on the far side of the pool (which is unusually big for this grade of hotel) the traffic can be heard whizzing along the *autoroute*. But that's a minor drawback to a rustic vacation among the horses.

DINING

Chez Loulou (E), Loew's Hotel (tel. 93–49–90–00). This luxury restaurant places much emphasis on lobster, caviar and the very best champagne, plus good simply grilled fish and impressive desserts. It's high quality, but the cuisine can't match the standard of the Oasis, see below.

L'Oasis (E), rue J.-H. Carle (tel. 93–49–95–52). Closed November through to mid-December, Monday evenings and all day Tuesday. Louis Outhier, of l'Oasis, ranks among the top ten of the gastronomic world's 30 or so best chefs. If you want to worship at this holy shrine of haute cuisine it is essential to book and to be carefree about the sordid matter of cash. It also helps to precede your visit by a prolonged period of fasting.

Outhier, born in 1930, worked first under the great Fernand Point before starting up here on his own in the '50s. His fame has been unchallenged for many years—but he worries. He worries about falling from grace, and so he works—you can see him in the kitchen with his lieutenant Jean-Pierre Meulin and 20 well-trained assistants. He works and works, he heeds criticism, he creates new edible delights. Among the mouth-watering specialties is *foie de canard au gingembre* (duck liver with ginger), a modern classic.

His dishes should be eaten rather than described, but rest assured you will be in good hands. Think in terms of 1,000 frs. for two to be on the safe side, though in 1987 it was possible, just, to dine well, sharing a bottle of the least expensive wine, for under 600 frs.

Other Restaurants. When you have an Oasis around, everything else pales into insignificance. But there are several other, less pricey, possibilities, all of them excellent when it comes to seafood. **La Brocherie II** (M), tel. 93-49-80-73, is at the port. Closed most of January, Monday evenings, and Tuesdays out of season. This one is real value for the dollar. Also at the harbor are **Le Lamparo** (M), **Le Bistrot** (I), again, both fine for fish.

NIGHTCLUBS

There is a mini-cabaret and dancing at **Loews,** in the Show Lounge bar. **Flash Dance** is a disco on the port. There are also a few other spots, but Cannes is the place for night life, and after all it's only five miles away.

SHOPPING

There's an open-air market on Wednesday mornings in the place de la Cascina, behind the Post Office, which is lively and fun. Otherwise the shops are nothing special—for something more exciting in the way of up-to-the-minute boutiques, wander into Cannes.

SPORTS

- **Fishing.** You don't need a license for sea fishing, but you do if you want to fish in either of the rivers that run through the town, the Argentière or the Siagne. Licenses are available from **Ryanne Sports** in the rue Guize.
- **Golf.** The two Cannes-Mandelieu courses—one 18 hole, the other nine—are right in the center of town by the sea. It is a delight to play on English turf, under

Mediterranean pines with, naturally, mimosa blooming here and there in spring. Visitors are welcome and coaching is available. (Tel. 93-49-55-39).
- **Horse Riding.** Just a couple of miles inland from Mandelieu-La Napoule on the N7, heading towards Fréjus, is the **Poney Club,** Domaine de Barbossi (tel. 93-93-14-18). This is a good place to take the kids, as it has a little zoo, and they can learn to ride the ponies. It is also a serious riding center for adults; horses can be hired, and there is tuition available.
- **Tennis.** There are numerous courts in the town, many of them offering coaching. Details are available from the tourist office.
- **Water Sports.** There are eight beaches for swimming, some public and some private. Waterskiing and jetskiing —for which there is a school on the plage du Sweet—are both easily arranged. If you want to go deep-sea diving, contact the **Club Nautique de l'Estérel,** Port du Rague. They offer lessons for anyone over the age of eight. Windsurfing equipment can be hired from **Sillages,** av. Henry Clews, opposite the château (tel. 93-49-10-10).

EXCURSIONS

There are excellent opportunities for inland walking here—though ideally you need the use of a car to get away from the town before you start. There are short walks or long walks, easy or arduous, through wild and rugged landscapes, or in among the lush vegetation of the forests. Several well-planned routes are marked by discreet blobs of paint on convenient rocks. Full details are available from the tourist office, which can also sell you a guide to day-long rambles in the Massif de l'Estérel.

There is a regular boat service, which usually runs twice a day from Easter through September, to the Iles de Lérins. See *Excursions* in Cannes for a full description. **Transports Maritimes Napoulois** (tel. 93-49-15-88) runs other sea trips.

This is a very good base for excursions by car, since so many other centers on the Riviera are within easy reach along the expressway. Grasse—see *Excursions* in Cannes for a description—is particularly easy to get to, using the D109 and D609 and returning via the lake of St.-Cassien.

Just to the west of town at **Maure-Vieil,** glassblowers create art glasswork and welcome visitors to their workshops and showroom.

Cannes

Cannes was a modest fishing village until the 1830s when a chance event changed its lifestyle forever. The story is part of the Cannes legend. In 1834 Lord Brougham, then Britain's Lord Chancellor, was en route for Nice when an outbreak of cholera forced the authorities to freeze all travel to prevent further spread of the disease. Trapped in Cannes, he fell in love with the place to such an extent that he bought a plot of land and built himself a house there as an annual refuge from the British winter. In the next few decades all the Best People—tsars, kings, and princes—were discovering Cannes. French Tourist Offices, who haven't yet learned to pronounce Brougham "Broom," refer to him as *milord*. He was in fact the first Lord Brougham, a brilliant, temperamental, self-made man and radical Whig politician, who fought for the abolition of slavery and for parliamentary reform among other controversial causes. He had an awkward personality—two of his nicknames were Beelzebub and Old Wickedshifts—but he knew a good place when he saw one.

Grand palace hotels were built to cater for the world's pre-1914 aristocracy and Cannes came to symbolize dignified luxury. The bright young things of the 1950s, who found it somewhat lacking in zip, deserted it for St.-Tropez, but nowadays Cannes has woken up. The young and lively are here in force in the summer and there are plenty of inexpensive hotels, pizzerias and cafés, and a vibrant nightlife. Cannes is also on the big business circuit and important conferences and conventions are held throughout the year. There are also various festivals, including the best known of them all—the International Film Festival.

Yet despite all this it is hard to escape the feeling that the real life of Cannes is still lived in the grand hotels, and that the most appropriate place to sun oneself is on an air mattress on a top-grade private beach below the Croisette. This can be achieved for around 100 frs. for the day, and to complete the Cannes experience lunch in a top hotel will cost twice that sum. You can do it on the cheap, but don't miss it altogether. It's attractive all year round and is still, as his lordship understood, a great place to spend the winter.

Exploring

The French have a word for it: *flâner* which means to dawdle, stroll, saunter, and this is the way to approach Cannes. Ignore any urges to go into the culture vulture routine. Relax and let the *esprit de Cannes* take control. First you should flâner along the famous mile-long **boulevard de la Croisette,** starting at the western end by the festival center (which has a multistory parking lot conveniently tucked away underneath it). To the right are the beaches, almost all of them private, but that doesn't mean you can't use them, only that you must pay for the privilege. They are graded, and the little life buoy symbols tell you their rating. They range from "two life buoys" to "four life buoys" according to the amount and quality of the equipment and facilities available, and the entrance fees vary also (from 30 frs. to 70 frs. for half a day in 1987). They all have restaurants or snack bars, and they all have lifeguards. The more expensive ones also provide masseurs, games, and facilities for snorkeling. On some, a ticket entitles you to eat lunch and use the beach all day. A few belong to the hotels on the other side of the road, but nonresidents are allowed to use them. The beach belonging to the great Carlton hotel, halfway along the Croisette, is open from March to October and has a glassed-in terrace and heating . . . so beach life can be continued even if the weather turns chilly.

The tourist office issues a plan of the beaches—*Les Plages de Cannes*—with full details and current charges.

The wide boulevard, with its palm trees and luxuriant flower beds, leads to the **Jardin Alexandre III,** and then continues in a more restrained form to the **Cap de la Croisette.** Here stands the Palm Beach summer casino, and from here you get a sweeping view to the east towards Cap d'Antibes.

Flâner back along the boulevard to the place du Général de Gaulle. For a change, walk on the other side (crossing with care, cars are the curse of the Croisette) to get a closer look at the smart hotels, shops, and cafés. When you regain the festival center strike inland, crossing rue Faure; walk down rue Rougière and turn left onto rue Meynadier, which is blessedly traffic free. Here you will find a plethora of interesting shops, including some fascinating food places, a few with elegant 18th-century doorways.

At the end of rue Meynadier take a dog-leg turn left and right past the bus depot into rue Georges-Clemenceau, then turn right again into rue du Mont Chevalier. Here is **Le Suquet,** the old part of Cannes. Climb up to the late 16th-century Provençal Gothic church of **Notre-Dame de l'Esperance.** There's a fine view from up here, and you'll also find the only museum in Cannes, the **Musée de le Castre,** in the remains of what used to be a castle. It is an ethnographical and archeological museum with statues, armor, pictures, porcelain, textiles, and ritual objects from all over the world. To step out of old Cannes, into an old castle, and come face to face with an Aztec god is to understand the meaning of culture shock.

Head downhill and you will find the main port, intensely busy in summer with luxury yachts, fishing boats, and merchant ships jostling each other on the water. Shops, restaurants, and cafés sit elbow to elbow on the quaysides. From here you can look across to the festival center where the tour began.

On a fine day, drive or take a bus or taxi (it's three miles away) to the **Observatory** at Super-Cannes. From 10 till dusk an elevator will take you up to the top of the tower. The view from it is truly panoramic, with the Alps and the Italian coast on one side, the Estérel on the other and, on a really clear day, Corsica out towards the horizon.

INFORMATION

- **Tourist Offices.** There are tourist offices at the railway station, the Gare SNCF, (tel. 93–99–19–77), and in town at the festival center at the western end of the Croisette, Palais des Festivals, 1 La Croisette (tel. 93–39–24–53). These are also **Accueil de France** offices where reservations can be made up to eight days in advance for hotels anywhere in France. Bear in mind that there is a charge for the telex, but that deposits are refundable. The tourist office also publishes monthly bulletins of events, in English.
- **Car Hire. Avis,** 69 La Croisette (tel. 93–94–15–86). **Europcar,** 3 rue du Commandant Vidal (tel. 93–39–75–20). **Hertz,** 147 rue d'Antibes (tel. 93–99–04–20).
- **Boat Hire.** Anyone who has a yen to get out on the Mediterranean should contact the **Yacht Club de Cannes,** Palm Beach Port (tel. 93–43–44–63). The experts there will be able to help you with advice on small boat sailing in the area. There's nothing quite like a lazy day's trip from Cannes to the Iles de Lérins, or along the coast to Monte Carlo or St.-Tropez. If you want to go for something larger than a small sailboat, you might contact **Northrop and Johnson,** 13 rue Pasteur (tel. 93–94–20–08). The company also has an office in the U.S. at Suite 210, South Harbor Plaza, 1300 Southeast 17th St., Fort Lauderdale, FL 33316 (tel. 305–523–5426).

If you can take the time, one week is just about right

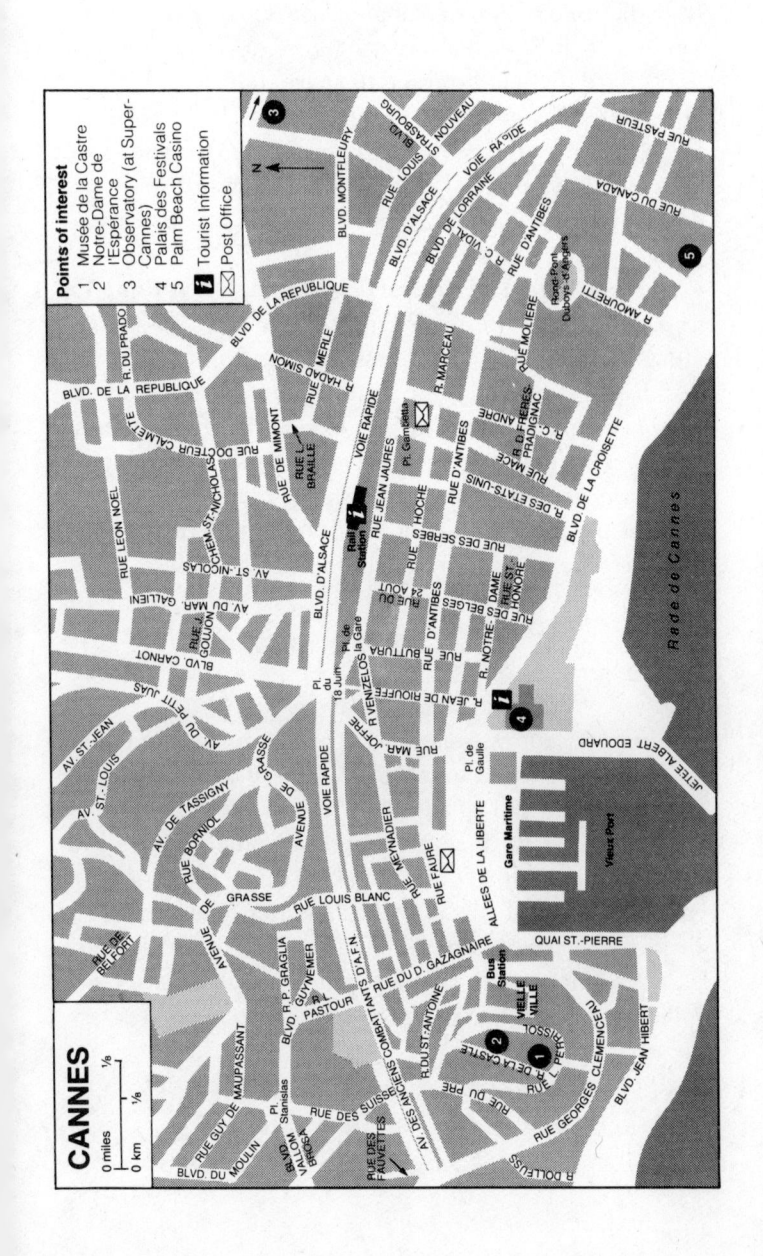

CANNES

for a leisurely cruise back and forth along the coast. Ten days would give you time to browse along the Italian Riviera, to Portofino or Rapallo, as well. You might even be able to include the crossing to Corsica. But if you don't have that kind of time to spare, then a fast motor-boat will get you to St.-Tropez for lunch. Motorboats also generally offer more space than sailboats, and more luxury. What's more they don't lean over and spill your drinks. But the choice depends entirely on your experience, preference, and life-style.

● **Waterskiing and Windsurfing. La Club Nautique La Croisette,** plage Jardin Pierre Longue (tel. 93–43–09–40), should be able to help anyone wanting to waterski. Windsurfers are rented at many sports shops all along the coast, and at most beaches. Rental charges are about 65 francs an hour, lessons are also available. Five minutes on waterskis will run just under 100 francs.

● **Post Code.** The post code for Cannes is 06400. It must be used when writing to any address in Cannes.

ACCESS

Getting to Cannes presents no problems at all. Those arriving by car need to know that the turnoff on the A8 highway is two and a half miles from the Croisette, while the N7 coastal road passes straight through Cannes. All express trains stop at Cannes; taking the night train from Paris is a romantic way to make an entrance. The nearest airport is at Nice, some 17 miles away. From there bus services connect with Cannes. There are also taxis available, as well as other road and rail connections between the two towns.

See under *Nice* for the availability of helicopter services.

HAPPENINGS

Cannes, despite its expansion during the 19th century, is still only a modest-sized town of 73,000 inhabitants. But its year-long programme of events is aimed at amusing and amazing many times that number.

Cannes is more or less synonymous with the International Film Festival, that glamorous event which fills it to the brim every May with the famous, the would-be famous, and the obscure who like to gaze upon the famous. Some of the world's top film stars can be spotted by the pilgrims, in the flesh; and starlets, who long to be spotted by producers, display all the flesh they can to the snapping photographers. The producers, meanwhile, are throwing parties for each other and the critics are creeping from one film to the next throughout the weary day. Hotel rooms have to be booked well in advance and the highest prices paid, and parking places are at a premium. Possibly the best way to handle a visit at this time is to visit Cannes from somewhere else along the railway line. The station is a bare quarter-mile from the Croisette and the Palais des Festivals.

The hubbub of the Film Festival may not appeal to everyone, but Cannes succeeds in putting on many other attractions throughout the year, with a slight lull during November and around Christmas. There are sports events and concerts, and massive firework displays at every excuse, with July 14 and August 15 the most lavish. Two other major media events are the International Records and Music Publishers' Market (MIDEM) in January, and in April, the International TV Programs Market (MIPTV), which draws the celebrities of the small screen as surely as the Film Festival draws those from the wide screen.

LODGING

Martinez (L), 73 La Croisette (tel. 93–68–91–00). 420 rooms. Closed mid-November to mid-December and February to mid-March. Today some of the luxury palace hotels that cosseted kings—the vast Metropole, the Hôtel du Parc, the Hôtel des Anglais—have receded into history. The Martinez, though, is still able to capture that sybaritic atmosphere of indulgence, even though it was not built until the '20s, a little late for classic status.

In 1982 the Concorde group, whose flagship is the magnificent Crillon in Paris, bought it, installed the dynamic Richard Duvachelle as manager, and spent 74 million frs. (about $12 million) revamping it. Duchavelle had it decorated in the style of the '30s but with all the luxuries of the '80s (heated swimming pool, sound proofing, air-conditioning). He also persuaded Christian Willer to move in as chef. Willer had been in charge of the Auberge des Templiers, a gourmet's mecca at Les Bizards, and he has raised the Martinez's two restaurants (one (E), one (M), see *Restaurants* below) to gourmet status. Today, even the buffet lunches served on the private beach are worthy of his name.

The tariffs are likely to leave the average person severely out of pocket, but some sensible package deals can drop prices almost to the (M) level. Six nights half-pension, which includes breakfast, lunch or dinner at the Orangerie (*à la carte* or by the pool), a mattress and parasol on the private beach, and an hour's tennis a day, was 3,870 frs. per person, sharing a double room, in 1987 (but 4,980 frs. in August)—*plus* 600 frs. for a room on the Croisette side. Without the daily Orangerie meal the price was 2,940 frs.

Hotel Gray d'Albion (L), 38 rue des Serbes (tel. 93–68–54–54). 200 rooms. Open all year. The Hôtel Gray d'Albion was not built until 1981, but in keeping with the Cannes penchant for luxury hotels, it's the last word when it comes to upmarket and up-to-date comfort.

Outside it is strikingly modern, totally white with angled ribs running the height of the façade. Inside, it is lush in that slick contemporary way which combines cool colors —grays and creams—with leather, metal, and mirrors. Located on a street leading to the sea the hotel is only 100 yards from the Croisette and is close to both the Casino and the Palais des Festivals. A fair sprinkling of celebrities is usually to be found enjoying the public rooms. There are three restaurants: the gastronomic **Le Royal Gray; Les 4 Saisons,** which serves international cuisine; and the restaurant-cum-club-cum-disco, **Le Jane's,** which offers a somewhat psychedelic experience.

In summer, guests can also use the private beach, which has yet another eatery. Rates, of course, vary with the season. A single room costs from 500 to 1,000 frs., a double from 600 to 1,100 frs., while those seeking to splurge out can book a suite in the high season for a mere 3,900 frs. a night.

There are three other luxury establishments which have successfully inherited the 19th-century mantle of the palace hotels. The blue-blooded aristocracy may have ceased to use Cannes as a playground, but today's silver-screen aristocracy still flocks here to enjoy the same high quality service once meted out to tsars and princesses.

Carlton (L), 58 La Croisette (tel. 94-97-04-21). 355 rooms. Open all year.

Grand (L), 45 La Croisette (tel. 93-38-15-45). 75 rooms. Open all year.

Majestic (L), 6 La Croisette (tel. 93-68-91-00). 300 rooms. Closed mid-November to mid-December.

Le Fouquets (E), 2 rond-point Duboys d'Angiers (tel. 93-38-75-81). 10 rooms. Closed October 20 to December 20. Le Fouquets is only five minutes from the sea, the Palais des Festivals, and the shops, yet it is located in a quiet residential area. It has a welcoming atmosphere and a decor of warm colors and rich French flounces. Each of the spacious rooms is air-conditioned and has a covered loggia. There is no restaurant, but that doesn't present a problem because there are several excellent ones nearby, including **Le Festival** or **Mère Besson.**

Hotel Gonnet et de la Reine (E), 42 La Croisette (tel. 93-38-40-00). Open April through October. This, the least expensive of the surviving examples of the Victorian palace hotels, has a splendid view. Its lack of air-conditioning and other modern doodads is somehow all part of its charm—it is as though it is too dignified and well placed to concern itself with such matters.

Novotel Montfleury (E), 25 av. Beauséjour (tel. 93-68-91-50). 81 rooms. Open all year. One of the Novotel chain, the hotel is modern, air-conditioned, sound-proofed, and obviously deeply concerned about the physical fitness of its clientele—there is an aerobic room, a sauna, tennis, and a heated swimming pool in the garden. There are sea views from the topmost floors but the location, though attractive, presents a problem to anyone without a car—it's in a ten-acre park a good 20-minutes' walk from the Croisette. It's smart and reliable but you could be almost anywhere.

Beau Séjour (M), 5 rue des Fauvettes (tel. 93-39-63-00). 46 rooms. Open mid-December to November. Just five minutes' walk from the sea and to the west of the main port, this hotel is modern and well-equipped, with a pleasant garden, swimming pool, air-conditioning, a more than adequate restaurant, and a garage.

La Madone (M), 5 av. Justinia (tel. 93-43-57-87). 24 rooms. Open all year. Some of the rooms here have kitchenettes which means you can cut the cost of your stay by catering for yourself. The setting is charming, in a leafy garden planted with palm trees and mimosa, with its own swimming pool and car park. The Pierre Canto Port end of the Croisette is no more than a ten-minute stroll away.

Les Dauphins Verts (I), 9 rue Jean-Dollfuss (tel. 93-39-45-82). 17 rooms. Open early January to December. As the hotels become cheaper so they become simpler. Nevertheless this one has air-conditioning in every room, private bathrooms, a garden, and a parking lot.

Festival (I), 3 rue Molière (tel. 93-39-69-45). 17 rooms. Closed all December. Some of the rooms have kitchenettes and fridges. The Festival is handily sited in the tangle of streets just behind the Palais Croisette.

Wagram (I), 120 rue d'Antibes (tel. 93-94-55-53).

CANNES

23 rooms. Closed January and February. This functional, inexpensive, hotel is very conveniently situated close to all tourist attractions. Be warned that not all the rooms have a private bath, but that isn't unusual for hotels in this price bracket on the Continent.

DINING

Royal Gray (E), Hôtel Gray d'Albion (tel. 93-68-54-54). Closed Sunday evenings and Mondays. Cannes's best restaurant, under Chef Jacques Chibois, who offers a fine—if expensive—*carte* and a delectable *menu dégustation* (tasting menu) of ten little dishes: this opens with *foie gras* on purslane salad with port jelly and truffle juice, and then guides the palate gently through a couple of hours of succulent surprises. For a more traditional meal, address yourself to the six course menu with that wonderful *foie gras* again, scallops with Beluga caviar, lobster in a Beaumes de Venise sauce, and tender morsels of lamb with a Provençale gratin of potatoes. For a lunch designed to keep anyone going, at least until dinner time, there's the *déjeuner d'affaires,* or business lunch, which brings to your table three courses of elegantly presented Chibois food and a carafe of wine—a culinary treat that falls nicely into the (M) category. Do book well in advance, and if the weather is fine, ask for a table on the terrace. (Unlike the hotel, the restaurant also closes in February and early March—top chefs need a chance to find out what their rivals are cooking up.)

Palme d'Or (E), Hotel Martinez (tel. 92-98-30-18). Closed Mondays, Tuesday lunch, lunch in July and August; February and the first half of March; and from mid-November to mid-December. Here chef Christian Willer draws lavish praise from gourmets for his choice line in light, inventive *cuisine moderne,* interspersed with authentic Provençale dishes. Like Chibois at the Royal Gray, he, too, presents a dazzling *menu dégustation,* but only if all the diners at a table order it. Apparently the two master chefs keep a beady eye on each other—while visitors of limited means fantasize about having enough money to alternate daily between the two establishments, keeping an (increasingly bleary) eye on both. The decor salutes the early days of cinema with posters and photos of Clark Gable, Maurice Chevalier, and a grinning Groucho Marx among others on the walls, and genuine '30s furniture. (The *Palme d'Or* is the highest award of the Cannes Film Festival.)

La Mère Besson (M), 13 rue des Frères-Pradignac (tel. 93-39-59-24). In July and August only dinner is served, and the restaurant closes Sundays. Mother Besson's nephew, Yves Martin, cooks here now, producing a reliable range of Provençale dishes. Especially recommended is the *aïolo,* served on Fridays, a great dish of fish and mixed boiled vegetables in a deliciously thick garlic mayonnaise.

l'Orangerie (M), Hôtel Martinez (tel. 93-68-91-91). Closed 20 November to 20 January. For probably the best bargain in Cannes, look to the Martinez again. Though bigger than the Palme d'Or, and sharing chef Christian Willer with it, it is cheaper and simpler. There's a four-course menu with a wide choice, including tempting desserts, which—as in the Palme d'Or—includes a few of grandfather's favorites, like pig's trotters, boned, stuffed, and roasted on a purée of potatoes and Swiss chard. For the calorie counters there's a health menu, alleged to provide less than 600 of them. The *carte* is properly translated into English with none of those puzzling mistakes, which may be good for a laugh, but make ordering somewhat tricky.

La Poêle d'Or (M), 23 rue des Etats-Unis (tel. 93-39-77-65). This translates as the Golden Frying Pan and here, just a few steps off the Croisette, Bernard Leclerc roasts a pretty duck or two and also concocts more inventive dishes. His waffles, with their unusual sauces, are famous among the local population.

Au Bec Fin (I), 12 rue du 24 Août (tel. 93-38-35-86). Closed Saturday evening and Sunday. Located in a side street only a stone's throw from the festival center this genuine bistro serves home-style cooking to an appreciative crowd of regulars. In 1987 it was possible to eat well from the 60 frs. and the 75 frs. menus.

To discover more restaurants in the (I) range, pick

up the tourist office leaflet, which lists no less than 86, as well as 29 pizzerias and 36 snack bars, brasseries, and hamburger places.

NIGHTCLUBS

Blitz, 22 rue Mace (tel. 93-39-31-31). Open from 11 P.M.; closed Sunday. This has the lot: a cabaret, a restaurant, and dancing to all hours.
   Brummel's, 3 blvd. de la République (tel. 93-39-07-03). Open from 6 P.M. A cheerful piano bar that encourages singalongs. It's inexpensive.
   Cancan, 1 rue Négrin (tel. 93-39-71-33). Open from 10 P.M. A disco with the added attraction of pretty hostesses.
   Disco 7, 7 rue Rougière (tel. 93-39-10-36). Open all night. This one flaunts a good drag cabaret and the appropriate clientele, but, being Cannes, is classy with it.
   Jane's, 38 rue des Serbes (tel. 93-68-54-54). A restaurant, piano bar, and disco all together, in the respectable and distinguished Hôtel Gray d'Albion. Civilized fun.
   Palm Beach Casino, pl. Franklin-Roosevelt (tel. 93-38-25-00). What's the Riviera without a little flutter at the tables? This is the summer version of Cannes's casino (in winter it's in the new Convention Center), and is open from 8 in the evening until 4. If you don't feel like chancing your luck, then there's a great dinner dance and cabaret, which runs from 9 (ties for the guys, dresses for the gals *de rigueur*). The locale is quite something, with the big room opening onto a swimming pool—you can swim and have lunch in the daytime. There is also a jazzier version of all this rather staid fun in the **Jackpot** disco, which is in full swing from 10:30 until daybreak.
   Ragtime, 1 La Croisette (tel. 93-68-47-10). This one's for jazz lovers. The setting combines a restaurant and piano bar.
   Studio Circus, 48 blvd. de la République (tel. 93-38-32-98). Open from 11 P.M. The top spot in Cannes; celebrities, stars and starlets, tycoons and the beautiful people are admitted, but not necessarily everyone else.

Cabaret, noise that you wouldn't believe, a laser show and all that.

SHOPPING

The top shops in France are to be found in just three towns: Paris, Cannes, and Monaco—which isn't in France, but you wouldn't notice.

Top women's fashion is expensive with a capital "E," but very, very chic. Some shops to try are **Chanel,** on the Croisette at 5 (*mais naturellement*). Halfway along the Croisette, turn down the rue Amouretti to find **Alexandra Scherra** at the Rond-Point Duboys-d'Angers. **Cacharel** is not far away at 16 rue des Belges. A few thousand dollars buys a nice little evening gown **Chez Joy,** one of the boutiques at the Hôtel Gray d'Albion. **Révillon** is at 45 La Croisette while the equally splendid **St.-Laurent** is at 21 rue d'Antibes. Even if you're not buying, window shopping can be fun, and you never know what—or who—you might discover while browsing.

For men it's simpler. Depending on what—or whom—you want to look like, there's **Cerruti 1881** at 15 rue des Serbes, and **Christian Dior** and **Francesco Smalto** at the Hôtel Gray d'Albion. Along the rue St.-Honoré are **Versace** and **Uomo.** For a Burberry and some warm woolies, there's always **Old England** at 26 rue d'Antibes.

Shoe shops, perfumeries, and jewelers abound. If you need a piece of luggage to impress the doorman the best place is **L'Odysée,** at 100 rue d'Antibes. The **Cannes English Bookshop** is at 19 rue Jean de Riouffe.

If you have a kitchenette in your hotel room, or plans for a picnic, the best place for cheeses is **Agnese,** 114 rue d'Antibes; for superb bread try **Martinez** at 18 rue Meynadier, and for charcuterie, **Giry** at 15 blvd. Carnot. All kinds of groceries, including imported lines, can be bought at **La Côte d'Or** at 107 rue d'Antibes, while chocolates and other confectionary can be found at **Bruno,** 50 rue d'Antibes, and **Maiffret** in the same street, at 31.

The colorful **market** in Cannes takes place on allées de la Liberté, Saturdays 9 to 5; in Hauts de Cagnes, pl. du Château, Sundays 9 to 5.

EXCURSIONS

LES ILES DE LÉRINS

The boats of the **Compagnie Estérel-Chanteclair,** Gare Maritime des Iles (tel. 93-39-11-82), head to the islands of Ste.-Marguerite and St.-Honorat from the main port, near the festival center, throughout the year. In summer the ferries run every hour, or even every half hour, while in winter there are four or five crossings a day. Ste.-Marguerite is 15 minutes away and St.-Honorat, 30. Both trips are scenic and a joy in themselves.

All islands have special appeal, and usually the smaller they are the more attractive they are. **Ste.-Marguerite** is only two miles long and just over a half mile wide, so visitors can easily walk right around it, via its coastal path, in about three hours. It is remarkably well-wooded with giant eucalyptus trees, pines, and scented Mediterranean shrubs, and the short forest walks are well signposted. Those who need a chilling moment to add spice to such an idyllic setting may like to know that the "Man in the Iron Mask" languished in the island's fortress. This construction may lose a certain something, though, when present plans to turn it into a youth center for underwater exploration and sailing are complete.

St.-Honorat is even smaller: about a mile long and 400 yards wide. An hour can be spent very pleasantly, walking around the island through shady woods on a path overlooking the sea. There is a monastery here where the monks grow oranges and lavender, keep bees for honey, and—as monks will—make a liqueur. Parts of their buildings can be visited, and so can the old fortified monastery which was built from the 11th century onwards. Sunday High Mass at the abbey is at 10:45.

MOUGINS

Post code 06250; tourist office av. Mallet (tel. 93–75–79–13). A fortified hilltop town of 10,000 citizens, Mougins is a mere five miles inland from Cannes. The old town center is picturesque and worth a look, but Mougins' main claim to fame is as a place of pilgrimage for gourmets. Here the celebrated Roger Vergé presides over **Le Moulin de Mougins** (E), at Notre-Dame-de-Vie (tel. 93–75–78–24). One of *the* places to eat on the Riviera, Le Moulin lies about a mile and a half out of Mougins along D3. Vergé has here created one of the very best restaurants in France, with a decor that is extremely luxurious, fine porcelain tableware, and an atmosphere which tells you that you are dining in one of France's Temples to Taste. The maître endlessly creates new dishes, like a master playwright always at work on a new script. He uses all the very best and most tasty local ingredients, creating some superbly simple dishes, as well as others that rank in the billionaire's favorite lobster-and-caviar category. If you are overcome with the deliciousness of the food, you could always bed down for the night in one of the five available guestrooms. Needless to say, the (E) rating points towards the stratosphere.

As often happens, the existence of one top restaurant stimulates competition, and today Mougins is a foodies paradise where you are unlikely to be disappointed by any meal. Other restaurants include:

L'Amandier de Mougins (E), pl. Lamy (tel. 93–90–00–91). Closed Wednesdays and Saturdays at lunchtime, and January to mid-February. Also under the watchful eye of Roger Vergé, but with lower prices than Le Moulin, this lovely old converted mill has itself won high marks from the critics. It can offer great views as well as delectable food.

La Ferme de Mougins (M), 10 av. St.-Basile (tel. 93–90–03–74). Closed mid-November to mid-December, mid-February to mid-March, and Monday and Thursday lunchtime. Not quite in the same class as the two previous ones, but still very acceptably rated in the gastronomic stakes. The spacious terrace makes for very relaxed summer eating. Excellent value in its range.

Le Feu Follet (I), pl. de la Mairie (tel. 93–90–15–78). Closed Sunday evening and Monday. Very satisfying food, with no pretensions and served with no fuss.

SHOPPING

Like the good entrepreneur he is, Roger Vergé hasn't finished with you after you have eaten at one or other of his magnificent restaurants. He also runs a food boutique in the village square—**Boutique du Moulin**—to give you the chance to take home a little bit of Riviera culinary magic.

GRASSE

Postcode 06130; tourist office, 3 place Foux (tel. 93–36–03–56).

Follow your nose down the N85 for five miles to Grasse, the town that calls itself the Perfume Capital of the World. A good proportion of its 38,000 inhabitants work at distilling and extracting the scent from the tons of flowers produced here every year, to create aromatic essences which will be blended into perfumes in Grasse itself or in Paris. The various perfumiers are only too happy to guide visitors around their fragrant establishments, to encourage them to sniff the product, and to help them to learn something of its preparation. Try **Fragonard,** 20 blvd. Fragonard (tel. 9–36–44–65), near the tourist office, for an expert guided tour of a perfume factory. There is also a shop to tempt your newly trained nose.

The old part of town is interesting, with its narrow alleys and massive somber cathedral. Three of the paintings inside are by Rubens and one by Fragonard who lived and worked here for many years. The ancient dwellings, though, are not occupied by artists, intellectuals, or summer visitors, but by the local working class and unemployed. The picturesque here verges on the run-down.

Take a look at the **Fragonard Villa Museum**, 23 blvd. Fragonard (tel. 93-36-44-65), in the 17th-century mansion where the artist stayed during the French Revolution. There is a Fragonard room upstairs, but other painters of the same period are also represented here. Open 10 to 12, 2 to 5, Monday to Friday, plus the first and last Sundays in the month.

Queen Victoria spent several winters in Grasse, in a palace-hotel that has long since been converted into apartments. There are hotels and restaurants in the town, but none of note. Many of the inhabitants, when they want a good lunch and an afternoon out, take the seven and a half miles along the N85 to St.-Vallier-de-Thiey.

ST.-VALLIER-DE-THIEY

Postcode 06460. This unassuming village has some good inexpensive restaurants and hotels, and is located in the midst of fine, wild, open country. At 2,375 feet above sea level, it is a complete change from low-lying coastal resorts. The little tourist office produces an excellent booklet (in French only) of recommended rambles, which range from a sedate post-prandial perambulation to a more athletic trek with spectacular views of the nearby forests and mountains. The hotel **Le Préjoly** (M), tel. 94-42-60-86, is good, with a restaurant in the (I) and (M) ranges. If full, there are other more inexpensive but perfectly adequate hotels. A day trip up here provides the perfect relaxing antidote to the sophisticated temptations of Cannes.

Antibes and Juan-les-Pins

One way to look at Antibes, Juan-les-Pins, and Le Cap d'Antibes is as a family group. Antibes itself represents the elderly parent—its history does, after all, go back to the 4th century B.C. when it was a Greek trading port. It still has serious business with the sea—the fishing boats go out most days—but its chief commercial activity now is the growing of roses and other fragrant flowers. It offers a graceful welcome to visitors, but remains at least partly preoccupied with its own pursuits.

Cap d'Antibes is the beautiful, wealthy daughter—a lusciously wooded rocky peninsula extending into the Mediterranean to the south, with elegant villas planted amongst the subtropical vegetation, spectacular views, and one of the most luxurious hotels to be found anywhere in France.

Juan-les-Pins is the raunchy youngster, north of the Cap and west of Antibes but touching both. Juan-les-Pins stays up all night having fun, drinking cocktails in open-air cafés, dancing, gaming in the casino, and still having enough youthful exuberance left over to keep the beaches lively all day.

For the summer visitor, Juan-les-Pins is the place for

immoderate fun at moderate cost; Cap d'Antibes for the quiet sweetness of Mediterranean life, at a price; old Antibes for picturesque charm all the year round, and perhaps especially in winter when Juan-les-Pins is sad and deserted, and the rich have temporarily abandoned their villas on Cap d'Antibes.

Exploring

The old town of Antibes is an amiable and pleasant place to wander around at any time of year, but from early spring through summer, when all the houses are decorated with brilliantly colored flowers, it is especially engaging. Start at the tourist office in the place de Gaulle and take a gentle stroll down the rue de la République towards the place Nationale, keeping an eye open for the rue James Close which leads off to the right. Here the interesting little shops are worth an hour of anybody's time, and there are several small but seductive restaurants.

There are more restaurants in the place Nationale itself, together with pavement cafés. A dedicated flâneur could spend all day sitting around here, watching life go by, occasionally being entertained by an open-air concert.

The rue Sade, which passes the place Nationale on the south side, leads down to the marketplace—the place Masséna. Go in the morning when the **market** is in full swing and meat, fish, glossy vegetables, and armfuls of flowers are changing hands in a general bustle of activity, and all in a haze of that special market smell. If you're into genre snapshots, this is definitely the place.

Leave the market by the rue de la Paroisse and you will come upon the **Church of the Immaculate Conception.** The fine wooden door with its intricate carving dates back to 1710, and the eastern end of the church is even older—the remains of a medieval cathedral. The altarpiece in the south transept chapel is by Louis Bréa and its date is thought to be 1515.

65 ANTIBES AND JUAN-LES-PINS

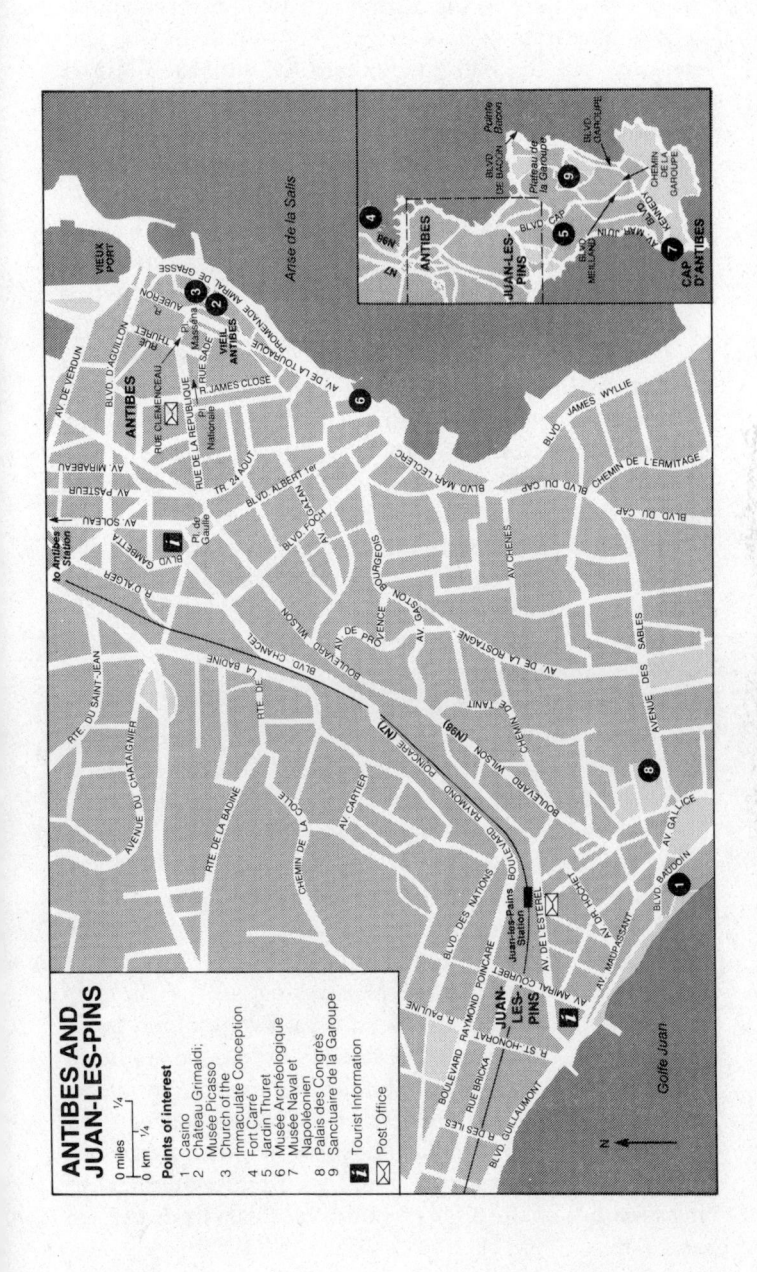

ANTIBES AND JUAN-LES-PINS

Points of interest
1. Casino
2. Château Grimaldi; Musée Picasso
3. Church of the Immaculate Conception
4. Fort Carré
5. Jardin Thuret
6. Musée Archéologique
7. Musée Naval et Napoléonien
8. Palais des Congrès
9. Sanctuaire de la Garoupe

i Tourist Information

⊠ Post Office

Outside, ascend some steps to the **Château Grimaldi.** The Grimaldis—the family that rules Monaco—built their castle here in the 12th century, on the remains of a Roman camp. It was extensively rebuilt in the 16th century, but the battlements and the sunbaked terrace overlooking the sea are original. Inside is a combination of museum and art gallery, with temporary exhibitions up on the second floor, and Roman pottery and stelae at ground level, but the chief attraction is the Picasso collection. The municipality placed the château at the disposal of that extraordinary genius, for a season, at a time when he was at his most cheerful and full of creative energy. The result is this bounty of exhilarating paintings, ceramics, and lithographs, inspired by the sea and by Greek mythology—all very Mediterranean. Even those who are not great fans of his style enjoy this show. The museum is open from 10 to noon and 3 to 6 daily, except Tuesdays, public holidays, and during November. In summer it opens an hour later in the evenings.

On leaving the museum, face the sea, turn right, and walk along the avenue de l'Amiral de Grasse, which follows the ramparts and overlooks the sea. After about ten minutes of enjoyable walking, you will find the **Musée Archéologique** in the St.-André Bastion. The collection of artefacts, dug from out of the land or fished up from the bottom of the sea, is continually being expanded as new items come to light, and covers 4,000 years of local history. The spoils from an Etrusco-Phoenician ship—wrecked off Cap d'Antibes some 2,600 years ago and not recovered until the 1950s—are the most dramatic, and the most disquieting in their reminder of long past tragedy. The Musée Archéologique has the same opening times as the Château Grimaldi.

Return to the market, place Masséna. Use the avenue de la Toureque for speed or, if in the mood to be sidetracked, take one of the flowery little pedestrianized streets—the rue du Haut Castelet, the rue du Bas Castelet, or the rue du Safranier. From the market place follow the rue Aubernon which wends its way down to the old harbor where **Fort Carré** stands guard over an interesting area full of the sights, sounds, and smells of the sea and boats.

JUAN-LES-PINS

If you want to take a look at Juan-les-Pins, follow the boulevard Wilson from the place de Gaulle, right across the neck of the peninsula to the seafront. Juan-les-Pins has fine sandy beaches, both public and private, and it also has a nightlife to beat all, throbbing and glittering its way in and out of the hotels, restaurants, cafés and pizzerias, the casino, and the multiplicity of lively nightclubs. If you are looking for that particular kind of brash, noisy fun that is supposed to be the Riviera's trademark then here is where to find it. The seal was set by Scott Fitzgerald, when he placed his *Tender is the Night* here.

However, if the beach bores and the nightlife sounds too much like hard work, then give it a miss and consider Cap d'Antibes.

CAP D'ANTIBES

The Cap d'Antibes peninsula is hardly two miles long by a mile wide, rocky, wooded, with the sea on three sides, and extravagantly beautiful. It offers a perfect day's outing—a comfortable dawdle punctuated by dips in the sea and pauses for snoozing in the Mediterranean sun, and with several opportunities for a delectable, if pricey, lunch.

It is possible to walk right around the outer edge, using *le sentier de douaniers*, the custom officers' footpath, but there are attractions worth visiting in the middle—if such a narrow outcrop can be said to have a middle.

Start from old Antibes, traveling clockwise, and the path soon reaches the **Pointe Bacon.** This is a wonderful vantage point from which to look back at Antibes and behind that to Nice and beyond. Here at the pointe is the **Restaurant Bacon** (tel. 93–61–50–02), a place of pilgrimage for those discerning fish eaters whose wallets can stand the strain.

Turn inland here and walk uphill to the **Plateau de la Garoupe** where the view is even more spectacular. The *table d'orientation* confirms that it extends all the way to the Estérel and to the Alps. There is also a lighthouse here—**Phare de la Garoupe**—whose beam extends for more than 40 miles across the sea and to a height of over 30,000 feet. There are guided visits from 10:30 to 12:30 and from 2:30 to 7:30 in summer, and to 5 the rest of the year.

The **Sanctuaire de la Garoupe** has a statue of Our Lady of Safe Homecoming (Notre-Dame-de-Bon-Port), the patron saint of sailors, and some touching votive offerings brought by sailors and their families to earn her protection. In early July the statue spends a few days in the church in Antibes and is then carried in a procession back to La Garoupe.

Not far away is the **Jardin Thuret,** a 17-acre garden established by the botanist Thuret, in 1865, to introduce new subtropical species to France. Its success was such that many of the plants that first tried out the French climate here are now quite common throughout the South. Among other things, the garden boasts France's first eucalyptus trees, brought here from Australia. It is open from 8 to 12:30, and 1:30 to 5:30, Monday to Friday, and closed weekends and public holidays. Close by are the **Meilland rose nurseries,** where new varieties are constantly being created.

The **Musée Naval et Napoléonien** is down at the southwest end, its gates facing those of the Hôtel Cap d'Antibes. A pair of bronze cannon seem set to repel invaders, but go in anyway—for the price of a few francs —and bone up on Napoleonic history. The documents attract some, the model soldiers appeal to many, but almost everyone is beguiled by the intricate models of ocean-going sailing ships. The museum is open 10 to 12, and 3 to 7 in summer, closing at 5 the rest of the year; also closed Tuesdays, public holidays, and November.

If you are willing to spend some 500 or 600 francs, lunching at the hotel, see below, is definitely something to write home about.

From here the avenue Maréchal Juin leads back to Juan-les-Pins and a different sort of fun.

INFORMATION

- **Tourist Offices.** The main tourist office for Antibes can be found at 11 place Général de Gaulle (tel. 93–33–95–64); it's right in the town center near the bus station.

  At Juan-les-Pins the tourist office is at 51 blvd. Guillaumont (tel. 93–61–04–98), on the sea front.

  Both tourist offices are open seven days a week in high season, six days a week the rest of the year.
- **Post Code.** The post code for Antibes is 06600, for Juan-les-Pins 06160. They must be used when writing to any address in either center.
- **Car Hire. Avis,** 32 blvd. Albert ler, Antibes (tel. 96–34–65–15). **Europcar,** 26 blvd. Foch, Antibes (tel. 93–34–79–79). **Hertz,** 129 blvd. Wilson, Juan-les-Pins (tel. 93–61–18–15).
- **Bicycle Hire.** From the rail stations at both Antibes and Juan-les-Pins.
- **Boat Hire. Eurydice Service,** 3 traverse du 24 Août, Antibes. **Agence Clemot,** headquartered at 18 quai St.-Pierre, 06402 Cannes, has a branch at Antibes.

ACCESS

Both Antibes and Juan-les-Pins are easy to reach. There are regular bus and train services from all the main centers on the Riviera, and especially from Cannes and Nice. For those coming by car, the N7, which is the main coastal road, runs right through Antibes, while the A8 expressway has an exit three miles from its center.

HAPPENINGS

At Antibes and Juan-les-Pins, or Juantibes as some insist on calling it, March–April is the time for a vintage car rally, a festival of young classical music soloists, and an antiques fair. In May there is the Vine-Growers' Festival, designed to promote local wines, some of which are very good, and all of which are worth tasting. There is also an international bridge tournament. In June it's time for the sea festival, with its colorful regattas and traditional ceremonies, and a big gymnastic tournament. In July a celebrated international jazz festival draws the crowds, while August has the *Pyromusique,* an explosive form of *son et lumière* combining fireworks and music—and, by way of complete contrast, an open-air programme of classical music. September sees sales-time when, during the *braderie,* shops offer their surpluses at surprisingly low prices in unsurprisingly busy street markets. In October there is a highly entertaining festival of cartoons and animated films and a car rally. November is for the birds, with a major avian show.

If all this is not enough, Cannes and Nice—each offering a wide range of events and activities—are not far away, and there are frequent trains to both for those who prefer to avoid the anguish of summertime parking.

LODGING

● **Antibes**
Mas Djoliba (M), 29 av. de Provence (tel. 93–34–02–48). 14 rooms with bath or shower. Open all year, but restaurant (I) closed in winter. This is the best of all worlds for people who love Antibes but want to live it up occasionally at Juan-les-Pins. It's a farmhouse (that's what *mas* means), but unlike a typical farmhouse it has a heated swimming pool, a garden, and plenty of room to park. The beach can be reached in ten minutes' walk, and the centers of Antibes and Juan-les-Pins in a quarter of an hour.

Royal (M), blvd. Maréchal Leclerc (tel. 93–34–03–09). 43 rooms, most with private bath or shower. Open January through October. It's right on the seafront, and so not as peaceful as the Djoliba, but beach lovers need only stroll across the road for a swim or a day's sunbathing.

Other Hotels. In the narrow streets of the old town around the place Nationale there are some simple hotels in the (I) class with a quiet charm of their own. If you fancy a few economical nights in surroundings that seem real rather than touristy, collect the list from the tourist office. Out of season you'll be able to take your pick, but even in season you should find a room.

• Cap d'Antibes

Hotel du Cap d'Antibes (L), blvd. Kennedy (tel. 93–61–39–01). 100 rooms, 10 suites. Open April through October. Exclusive with a capital "E." The best of the past and the present combine in this splendidly modernized Victorian palace hotel, set in its own magnificent park which sweeps down to the seashore. If you feel rich enough to stay in an establishment where room service will deliver champagne to your bedside 24 hours a day as required, this is definitely the place for you. Outside there is an inviting swimming pool and well-appointed tennis courts, while inside valuable antique furniture stands about on marble floors. Yet another Scott Fitzgerald location, and now with a really splendid restaurant (see *Pavillon Eden Roc* below).

Motel Axa (E), blvd. de la Garoupe (tel. 93–61–36–51). 20 rooms with private bath. Open all year. This, too, is set in pleasant grounds and has its own swimming pool and tennis courts, but as each room has its own kitchenette you can cut costs by buying food in Antibes market and preparing your own Provençale feasts. No need to bother about breakfast, though, that's included in the price.

La Gardiole (M), chemin de la Garoupe (tel. 93–61–35–03). 21 rooms, with shower or bath. Open March through November. What, no swimming pool? No, but a good beach is only five or ten minutes' walk away. The hotel, in its pinewood setting, is peaceful and quiet, with a lovely terrace draped in wisteria, and an acceptable restaurant (I) that serves some excellent Provençale specialties.

• Juan-les-Pins

Belles Rives (L), blvd. Baudoin (tel. 93–61–02–79). 42

rooms. Open mid-April to early October. They say this was Scott Fitzgerald's favorite hotel. It is comfortable and endearingly old-fashioned, and though it has no pool this is no loss because the beach is nearby. Even allowing for the period charm of the place, it attracts a very upbeat, young clientele. Dining on the terrace, with its splendid views, is a delight.

Juana (L), av. Gallice (tel. 93–61–08–70). 50 rooms. Open mid-April to end October. This beautifully renovated '30s hotel is opposite the casino overlooking the public gardens. Its good swimming pool, private beach, and top restaurant (*La Terrasse,* see below) make it hard to beat. It is possible that the Juana will appeal especially to our older readers.

Les Mimosas (M), rue Pauline (tel. 93–61–04–16). 36 rooms. Open April through September. A quarter of a mile from the seafront, this hotel is a quiet refuge from the excitement of the summer goings-on. It has a swimming pool, flanked by shady palm trees, all set in a big garden. Every room has a terrace and a private bath.

Auberge de l'Estérel (I), 21 rue des Iles (tel. 93–61–08–67). 15 rooms. Open from mid-December through mid-November. Sited in a secluded garden, this is known mainly as a very good restaurant, but the rooms are peaceful, and a stay is highly recommended, especially to the budget conscious.

● **Out of Town**
Fimotel Neptune Antibes (M), 2599 route de Grasse (tel. 93–74–46–36). 75 rooms. Open all year. Convenient for drivers, who only need head down the expressway for about three miles out of Antibes to find the hotel. It's a modern establishment, efficient rather than charming, with a clean swimming pool, tennis courts, a garden, and a restaurant (I).

Novotel (E), Sophia Antipolis (tel. 93–33–38–00). 97 rooms. Open all year. This hotel and the one following are both in **Sophia Antipolis,** a purpose-built town about six miles from Antibes which has ambitions to become another Silicon Valley (it's the location of a scientific research park). This is not your typical Riviera fun center, but is well placed for explorations by car. One of a well-known chain, the Novotel offers the predictable luxuries—air-conditioning, a swimming pool, tennis courts, and a restaurant (I).

Ibis (M), Sophia Antipolis (tel. 93-65-30-60). 99 rooms. Open all year. The Ibis is a link in another hotel chain, but one which is considerably less expensive than the Novotel. Reliable if not atmospheric, it, too, has a restaurant (I).

The postal address for both hotels is Sophia Antipolis, 06560, Valbonne.

DINING

- **Antibes**

La Bonne Auberge (E), La Brague (tel. 93-33-36-65). Open daily except Mondays, seven days a week in July and August. Closed mid-November to mid-December. There are only 92 restaurants in France which rate two Michelin stars, and this is one of them. Jo Rostang and his son Philippe will knock your socks off, gastronomically speaking, and their wine cellar is superb. Philippe served his apprenticeship at l'Archestrate in Paris, and with the Troisgros Brothers at Roanne—gastronomes genuflect at the mention of either. The single snag is the location, two and a half miles north of Antibes, on the horrible N7 road, and near a railway line, but if the Rolls Royces and Porsches can make the trip, so can the rest of us—and, anyway, the restaurant is sound-proofed. Be sure to reserve your table—if you're lucky, you may even get one with a view of the inspired work going on in the kitchen.

Il Giardino (I), 21 rue Thuret (tel. 93-34-56-58). Simple and unpretentious, specializing in good homemade pasta and grilled meals with a distinctive Italian flavor. The locals *mange ici,* always a reassuring sign.

- **Cap d'Antibes**

Bacon (E), blvd. Bacon (tel. 93-61-50-02). Open Tuesday to Saturday, February to mid-November. The best restaurant on the Riviera for *bouillabaisse* or any other dish that depends on prime fish, simply and perfectly cooked. Fish are relatively scarce in the Mediterranean and most of the cheaper restaurants haul in frozen stuff from Senegal or Thailand, while the more expensive go for fresh fish from the Languedoc port of Sète. However, the Sordello brothers, who have run this place for 40 years, don't regard a fish as fresh unless it is still twitching, so here you will dine on the pick of the local catch, perhaps accompanied by a white wine from the Domaine Ott and followed by a dessert. Forget the langoustine, it's only here for the snobs. (If bad weather prevents the fishermen from netting the proper ingredients, the *bouillabaisse* will not reach the table—there are no compromises here). A reservation is essential.

Pavillon Eden Roc (E), Hôtel du Cap d'Antibes (tel. 93-61-39-01). Open daily from April through to October. Place your reservations here for a memorable Riviera experience—lunch beside the famous swimming pool with its equally famous view. The cuisine may not rise to the gourmet heights of others in the area, but the situation and surroundings are so glamorous that no one really cares.

● **Juan les Pins**
Les Belles Rives (E), blvd. Baudouin (tel. 93-31-02-79). Open daily from mid-April to early October. This one may not have won any Michelin stars, but nonetheless the classic cuisine is impeccably served and the setting is a delight. For best magical effect dine on the terrace on a fine summer's night, with the sea lapping below and the stars twinkling in the velvety Mediterranean sky. It's guaranteed to make any vacation into a honeymoon!

La Terrasse (E), av. Gallice (tel. 93-61-08-70 or 93-61-20-37). Open mid-April to end of October; during July and August dinner only is served. This is the restaurant of the Hôtel Juana and, like La Bonne Auberge, bears two Michelin stars. Panic set in among local gourmets when, at the end of 1986, the Hotel de Paris in Monte Carlo lured away that excellent chef, Alain Ducasse. But La Terrasse moved fast and acquired the young and talented Christian Morisset and a high octane sigh of relief was breathed over Juan-les-Pins. Dining by candlelight on the beautiful poolside terrace is an event to remember.

Auberge de l'Estérel (M), 21 rue des Iles (tel. 93–61–08–67). Open Tuesday to Sunday lunchtime, mid-December to mid-November. The Plumail brothers serve imaginatively prepared local food at such reasonable prices that, with a little attention to the menu, it is possible to bring the check down to (I) level. The secluded garden is an enchanting setting for an evening meal.

Other Restaurants. There are quite literally dozens of cheerful little restaurants in the area, both in (M) and (I) categories, serving well-prepared food. If you rely on serendipity for choice, you'll be very unlikely to go wrong.

Nightclubs

The nightlife in Juan-les-Pins is so intense and varied, and there are so many popular and lively nightclubs, that those seeking to get the most fun possible out of the hours of darkness are spoilt for choice.

Le Bureau, av. Georges Gallice, Juan-les-Pins (tel. 93–67–22–74). The dancing is particularly good at this one, the clientele young and buoyant. As with most clubs in the area, those pushing 40 from the other side may feel their age.

Le Crystal, av. Georges Gallice. Another rendezvous for the spirited and debonair, just down the road from Le Bureau. Cocktails are served on the terrace and there is a range of 53 different Continental beers.

La Siesta, route du Bord de la Mer, Antibes (tel. 93–33–31–31). Open summer only. Exactly the wrong name for an enormous set-up where you can do just about anything except sleep. There are no less than seven dance floors, bars, supper places, and roulette—all lit by dramatically flaming torches. It's packed on hot summer nights—you never know who you may meet, and there's always the chance you'll wake up on the beach next day.

Shopping

For beachwear and other such frivolities, try the shops along the sea front at Juan-les-Pins. They are open until 11 P.M. in season—but once the season closes, so do they.

For more elegant and varied shopping, take the train to Cannes, Nice, or Monaco.

Self-caterers and picnickers should go directly to the market in old Antibes, where choosing the food is almost as much fun as eating it. Numerous varieties of bread are on sale at **Guelpa,** 20 rue Clemenceau, and a splendid selection of cheeses scent the air at **l'Etable,** la rue Sade. The best wine selection is at **l'Arôme des Vins,** 15 blvd. Foch—while those who don't trust their own cooking should seek out **La Charcuterie Lyonnaise,** 21 rue de la République which has an especially good delicatessen, and a range of prepared dishes.

The Antibes **market** is held in the pl. Audebert in the Old Town, Thursdays 7 A.M. to 6 P.M., and Saturdays 8 to 6.

Excursions

Marineland (tel. 93-33-31-31), Europe's first aquatic zoo, is only a short way out of Antibes. Travel north along the N7 towards Nice for just under three miles, then turn left on to the D4, signposted to **Biot.** Marineland appears almost immediately on the right. Seals, sealions, and penguins are all incarcerated here for your pleasure, but it is the highly intelligent, permanently smiling dolphins that draw the crowds. They present acrobatic performances several times every afternoon, throughout the year. Last shows are at 5 in winter, 6 in summer, and 7:30 during July and August.

It is well worth continuing along the D4 to the picturesque village of Biot itself, where mimosa and roses are grown for the cut flower market. Once upon a time it was famous principally for the manufacture of pottery, especially for the big earthenware jars crafted by—wouldn't you know it—*jarriers*. Now it is just as well known for its glass, and the glassworks, at the edge of the village, welcomes visitors who can watch the traditional blowing process and, of course, buy if they wish. It's open most mornings and afternoons, but don't make a special trip without calling first, on 93-65-03-00.

The artist Fernand Léger (1881–1955) lived here, and the **Fernand Léger Museum** is at the south edge of the village, in a building designed by the Niçois architect A. Svetchine. The distinctive, stylized paintings, ceramics, and tapestries, given to the nation by the artist's widow, are arranged chronologically, so that it's easy to follow his development. The museum is open from 10 to 12, and 2 to 6 daily, except Tuesdays and some public holidays.

There are several satisfactory places to eat here. Especially friendly is **l'Auberge du Jarrier** (M), tel 93-65-11-68. If you plan to feast here, check first, because opening times are a little whimsical—daily, except Tuesdays and Wednesday lunchtimes in June through August, with closed periods in November, December, and March.

Mougins and Grasse, described in the previous chapter, can also be visited very easily from Antibes. Just head down the D35 for Mougins and turn off to the N85 for Grasse.

The Iles de Lérins, Monaco, and St.-Tropez are all served during high season by regular boat services—and any one of them is within easy day-trip reach. For details, check with the tourist office.

From antibes to nice

A 13-mile stretch of flat coast lies between Antibes and Nice. While on the N7, keep reminding yourself that Nice is not far away, and is a terrific place, and that turning inland just before you reach it will lead you to some enchanting places—because it has to be said that the road is severely lacking in charm. On one side is a dull gray, stony shore, with ugly concrete structures; on the other are more concrete structures and the railway line. The traffic is heavy and travels unpleasantly fast. But Nice and the hinterland justify the torture.

VILLENEUVE-LOUBET

Try the turn-off between Antibes and Nice to Villeneuve-Loubet. This attractive riverside village, dominated by a medieval château which is privately owned and not open to the public, is a place of pilgrimage for dedicated gourmets. It is the birthplace of Auguste Escoffier, he who invented Pêche Melba, and was probably the most famous and accomplished of France's master chefs. The house where he was born in 1846—to the local blacksmith and his wife—is now the **Musée Escoffier,** 3 rue Escoffier. Sacked from the London Savoy, for overdoing the traditional kickbacks from suppliers, he had no difficulty in moving on to Claridges and the Ritz in London, and also to the Paris Ritz. In the typical Provençal kitchen downstairs, marvel at the magnificent marzipan and sugar *pièces montées,* and then move upstairs to examine a few of the 15,000 menus. It is a sobering experience to spend time in a place devoted entirely to the worship of food but where there is nothing actually to eat. It's open from 2 to 6 daily except for Mondays, public holidays, and in November.

Beside Villeneuve-Loubet is Haut-de-Cagnes, with Cagnes-Villes, Cagnes-sur-Mer, and Cros-de-Cagnes adjoining. To avoid getting Cagnes confused with Cannes, bear in mind that Cannes is pronounced roughly "kan," while Cagnes is pronounced—even more roughly—"kine." The **Château** at Haut-de-Cagnes (tel. 93-20-85-57) is a splendid medieval fortress with an eclectic collection of works of art in its various rooms and a good view from the top of the tower. There are paintings by modern Mediterranean artists—Chagall and Seyssaud among them—wondrous fireplaces and ceiling paintings, and all that anyone could want to know about the history and uses of the olive. It is open 10 to noon and 2:30 to 7 in summer, 5 in winter; closed on Tuesdays, and from mid-October to mid-November.

Perched by the ramparts of Haut-de-Cagnes is **Le Cagnard,** a hotel famous among France's intelligentsia. It was converted out of several extremely ancient village houses, and is both luxurious and picturesque—not a usual combination. Simone de Beauvoir wrote *Les Mandarins* here. It has 19 rooms (though some of them are rather small), many with a private terrace and lovely view. It is closed from November to mid-December, and if you can't stay, try the restaurant to get some taste of the place's atmosphere. Le Cagnard (E), rue Pontis-Long, Haut-de-Cagnes (tel. 93–20–73–21). Post code 06800 Cagnes-sur-Mer.

ST.-PAUL-DE-VENCE

Penetrating farther uphill and inland you will come upon the picture-book village of St.-Paul-de-Vence, only ten miles from Antibes and 12 from Nice. A prosperous place in the Middle Ages, it gently declined afterwards until the 1920s when its visual appeal was discovered by painters, who made their base at its modest inn, **The Colombe d'Or.** Inevitably the little inn has come up in the world since, in a big way, and the one-time simple hideaway now has air-conditioning, a heated swimming pool, and a collection of valuable modern paintings, most notably by Picasso and Rouault. It has a restaurant (M) and a beautiful terrace where stars of stage and screen enjoy being recognized. Colombe d'Or, St.-Paul-de-Vence (tel. 93–32–80–02). Post code 06570 St.-Paul. It has 23 rooms and closes down from November to late December.

The village is very much on the tourist-trail, especially for day-trippers up from the coast, and almost every little house seems to be in the souvenir business. The streets are for pedestrians only, but their medieval narrowness means that they are often packed with people, speaking a dozen different languages. To enjoy the place at its best, arrive early, and have breakfast at the **Café de la Place** by the pétanque pitch.

Less than a mile from the village is the famous and unusual **Fondation Maeght** (tel. 93-32-81-63). This is a temple of modern art, an attractive architectural ensemble that fits in surprisingly well with the pinewood that is its setting. Giacometti's figures stride the courtyards and works by Calder, Zadkine, Chagall, Miro, and Braque are at home here. Inside are artists' studios, a library, cinema, and auditorium. Concerts and other events are held throughout the year and there are regular temporary exhibitions. If you want to write in advance for further details, the post code is 06570 St.-Paul. The center is open 10 to 12:30 and 3 to 7 from June through October. From July to September there is no midday break. In winter it closes an hour earlier in the evening.

A short distance away, in its own glorious 20-acre park, is an ideal luxury hotel for those in need of peace and relaxation. A long weekend at the **Mas d'Artigny** could be just what the doctor (or perhaps more specifically the psychiatrist) ordered. Savor smooth Rolls-Royce efficiency and huge quiet rooms with wide windows and terraces looking out on to the hills of Provence. There is a swimming pool, naturally, but you may decide to use your room's own private pool instead (26 garden suites have them). The managers, M. and Mme. Scordel, speak perfect English, and the restaurant (E) has a good chef, Anton Dorschner. A visit is worthwhile even if you don't stay there. Mas d'Artigny (L), (tel. 93-32-84-54). Post code 06570 St.-Paul. 56 rooms, and 29 suites. Open all year round.

VENCE

A couple of miles farther on is Vence. A quick drive through reveals a middle-sized town of no particular interest, but head for the old town, **la Vieille Ville,** and the appeal of Vence, in its luxuriant country setting, becomes obvious. It is easy to spend a happy hour strolling around the medieval ramparts and exploring the traffic-free streets of this charming place, which was founded by the Romans and which became an important bishopric in the 4th century with the cathedral on the site of the old Roman temple to Mars. During the religious wars it withstood a siege and it still celebrates this triumph every Easter.

Outside the "new town" is the **Chapelle du Rosaire,** conceived and decorated by Matisse between 1947 and 1951 as a gift to the nuns who had nursed him. It's a place of gentle genius, with a simple, light, happy atmosphere. It is open from 10 to 11:30 and 2:30 to 5:30 on Tuesdays and Thursdays, except public holidays.

Close by is **La Roseraie,** neither a rosary nor a rose garden but a really good restaurant (I) with a giant magnolia standing on its terrace. Chef Maurice Ganier comes from the southwest of France, and so do the ducks and geese that form the infrastructure of his cooking. Eating here is a cheering reminder that you don't have to be rich to have a good time. There are also nine rooms (M) should you want to stay over. La Roseraie, route de Coursegoules, (tel. 93–58–02–20). Open from mid-March to mid-October.

Vence **tourist office,** place du Grand Jardin, 06140 Vence, (tel. 93–58–06–38).

Nice

Nice is bustling and lively with its own university and industries and a population of 338,000, and a life that carries on happily independent of the tourist trade. Because of this there are plenty of moderately priced hotels, restaurants, and shops—as well as their more luxurious counterparts—and the town crackles with action all the year round and not only in season. In fact, during the peak vacation months of July and August some of the best restaurants close, preferring to reserve their energies for their regular customers.

Visitors may not be the *raison d'être* of Nice, but it is a deservedly popular holiday center with much to offer. Few who have stayed here would dispute its right to call itself "Queen of the Riviera." There is an interesting mixture of old and new architecture, an opera house, museums, flourishing markets, and regular concerts and festivals, including the famous Mardi Gras and the Battle of the Flowers.

The English who patronized Nice during the 19th century equipped it with a sweeping promenade which does much to compensate for the fact that the beaches are shingly and rather exposed.

Nice has not always been part of France. The arcades and red ocher colors in the older section are a reminder that the town belonged to Italy until the plebiscite of 1860 in which 25,743 people voted in favor of being French and a mere 260 voted against. At that time the population was only 40,000. The arrival of the railway was responsible for the town's growth to its present size, and the efficient train services, following routes all along the Riviera coastline, are one of the factors that make this an excellent starting point for excursions. There is also a major airport and a vast network of bus routes, carrying regular services from the Gare Routière all over this part of Provence. Between them, these facilities mean that a car is not an essential piece of holiday equipment.

Exploring

The logical starting point for an exploration of Nice is the **place Masséna.** Construction of this fine square began in 1815 and the name was chosen to celebrate the local hero, one of Napoleon's most successful generals. Victorious at the battles of Rivoli and Wagram, among others, Masséna finally met his defeat at the hands of Wellington in the Peninsular War.

The **promenade des Anglais** is only a short stroll past the fountains and the **Jardin Albert I.** Presented with a seafront that was hard to reach, and with plentiful cheap labor, the English community initiated the promenade in 1824. It has been widened over the years, and is no longer a true prom since it now carries heavy traffic, but it still forms a splendid strand between town and sea. Cross with care, at the traffic lights.

On the seaward side lie the private beaches. These are graded one to four, with life-buoy symbols instead of the customary stars. The more facilities a beach has to offer, the more life buoys it is accorded—and the more expensive it is to use. All the beaches have cabins, showers, and parasols, some have much more. The nearest,

Ruhl Plage, which merits four life buoys, has a good restaurant, waterskiing, parascending, and swimming lessons for children.

Beyond is the magnificent **Baie des Anges,** or Bay of Angels, with the **Neptune Plage,** a four life-buoy beach which has all the attractions of the Ruhl Plage and a sauna complex too.

It is well worth crossing the road at this point to the **Hôtel Negresco.** The doorman's uniform of plumed top hat, scarlet-lined blue cloak, and high boots is some indication of the splendor that is within. A cup of tea here costs 22 frs., but regard it as an entrance fee to an historical monument, and it's cheap at the price. See as much as you can of the public rooms, and don't neglect to visit the bathroom.

Continue along the hotel side of the promenade until you reach the **Musée Masséna.** The Napoleonic era, and especially Masséna and his family, are illustrated here with portraits and statues, and there are some fine altarpieces and an important collection of religious objects including a resplendent Italian Renaissance reliquary. The sections devoted to Nice and the Carnival offer a painless introduction to the history of the town. The museum opens daily, except Mondays, from 10 to noon and from 3 to 6, in summer. It closes an hour earlier in winter, and for two weeks in November and December.

From the inland side of the museum turn right into the rue de France, which soon becomes the rue Masséna. This area is pedestrianized and slightly touristy, but it has plenty of shops, and numerous pizzerias for inexpensive meals. The rue Masséna heads back to place Masséna.

To reach the old town, probably the most appealing part of Nice, turn south—or seawards—in the place Masséna, walk down the short rue de l'Opéra and then turn left into the rue St.-François-de-Paul. On your left you will see the **church of St.-François-de-Paul,** which dates back to 1750 and has an exuberantly Baroque interior. On the right is the glamorous **Opera House.** The famous tea shop, **Henri Auer,** is in this street—the crystallized

85 NICE

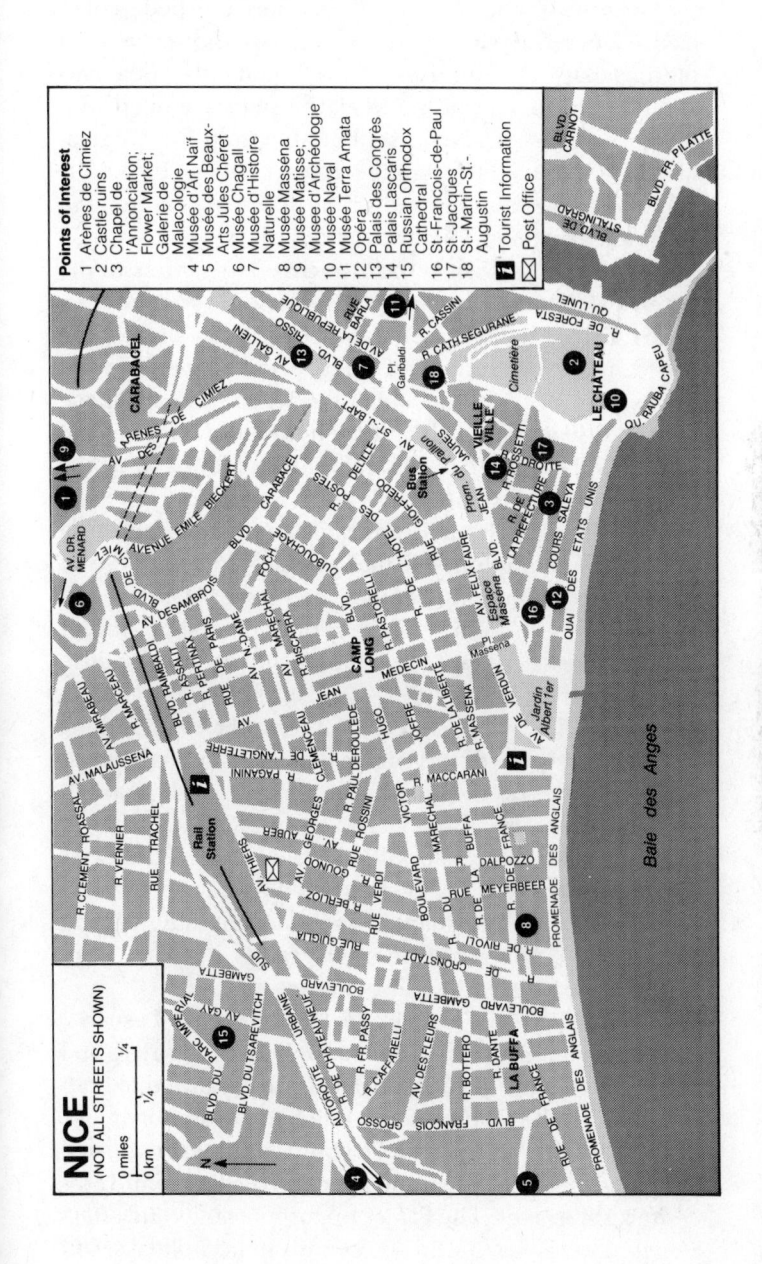

NICE
(NOT ALL STREETS SHOWN)

Points of Interest
1. Arènes de Cimiez
2. Castle ruins
3. Chapel de l'Annonciation; Flower Market; Galerie de Malacologie
4. Musée d'Art Naïf
5. Musée des Beaux-Arts Jules Chéret
6. Musée Chagall
7. Musée d'Histoire Naturelle
8. Musée Masséna
9. Musée Matisse; Musée d'Archéologie
10. Musée Naval
11. Musée Terra Amata
12. Opéra
13. Palais des Congrès
14. Palais Lascaris
15. Russian Orthodox Cathedral
16. St.-Francois-de-Paul
17. St.-Jacques
18. St.-Martin-St.-Augustin

i Tourist Information
✉ Post Office

fruit, rich ice creams, or delicious pastries are all worth tasting.

Rue St.-François-de-Paul becomes the pedestrianized **Cours Saleya** where the famous flower market blooms daily. On Mondays it's predominantly a flea market, but for the rest of the week the stalls are piled with produce—flowers, of course, but also fruit, fish, vegetables, and pretty little orange trees in tubs. Inevitably some of the restaurants and shops in this area are on the verge of becoming tourist-oriented.

Well worth a visit is the attractive little annex to the **Natural History Museum,** the **Galerie de Malcologie,** which displays a collection of seashells from all over the world, including rarities of unexpected shapes. Not all the exhibits are dead—some of the Mediterranean specimens cruise in high-tech tanks. The Galerie is open from 11 to 1 and from 2 to 6, closed Sundays, Mondays, public holidays, and November.

Stroll north from Cours Saleya, up the rue de la Poissonerie, and you will find yourself in a muddle of narrow streets and little squares, all pedestrianized and all bustling with local residents doing their shopping. A large scale street map, available from the tourist office, is a great asset here.

Before leaving the rue de la Poissonerie have a look at the **Chapel de l'Annonciation**—another florid Baroque interior gleaming with marble and polished paneling and with grand altarpieces in its Lady Chapel.

The large scale map will assist you to the **Eglise-St.-Jacques,** at the east end of the rue du Jesus. Walk inside, wait for your eyes to adapt to the dim church light, then raise them to the ceiling where the saint's life story is set out in an explosion of painted scenes.

Nearby, in the rue Droite, is the **Palais Lascaris.** This small but elegant palace was built between 1643 and 1650 for Count Jean-Baptiste-Lascaris-Vintimille, descendant of the Count of Vintimiglia and of a daughter of the Lascaris, 13th-century Byzantine emperors. Inside are paintings, tapestries, and a reconstruction of an 18th-century pharmacy. The Palace opens mornings and afternoons, but closes Mondays, some public holidays and during November. Guided tours of the old town set out from here.

Wander on, past bakers' and butchers' shops, to the charming place St.-François with its fountain and morning fish market, and continue northwards to another attractive Baroque church, the **Eglise-St.-Martin-St.-Augustin.** Here, Martin Luther celebrated mass at the altar and Garibaldi was baptized at the font.

Continue north and almost at once the narrow streets are left behind and the grand place Garibaldi opens out—all yellow ocher buildings and formal fountains—lying at the northern extremity of the old town. This may be the time to make an emergency stop for a dozen oysters and a pitcher of white wine. If so, head for the **Grand Café de Turin** (see *Restaurants* below); though if there isn't an "R" in the month some other snack will have to do.

A famous landmark that can't be ignored is the Castle Hill, **la Colline du Château,** the romantic cliff that can be seen from so many parts of Nice, especially after dark when its waterfall is floodlit. The best approach is along the rue des Ponchettes, which runs across the south of the old town. The hill was first fortified many centuries before the birth of Christ, but its ruins are those of a 16th-century castle, destroyed in the 18th century. The flamboyantly fit jog up the 400 steps; the rest of the world opts for the elevator, *l'ascenseur.* This operates from 9 to 8, June through August, stops at 7 during all the other months, and runs afternoons only from mid-October to mid-March.

Near the elevator exit at the top is the naval museum, **le Musée Naval,** in the upper part of the Bellanda Tower, where Berlioz once lived. Here are models of ships and of the port of Nice at various stages of its development, and complex instruments of navigation. The museum opens the same hours as the elevator, but with a two-hour lunch break from 12:30. It is closed on Tuesdays and public holidays.

Follow the winding path to the top of the hill, above the waterfall, and enjoy spectacular views over Nice and the Bay of Angels from 300 feet above them. A conveniently placed viewing plan ensures that the principal sights don't remain anonymous.

If you prefer a different route down, follow the signposts to **Cimetière** and **Vieille Ville,** and the path will lead you to the old town.

There are two more avenues which should be explored, both leading from the place Masséna. The first is the avenue Jean-Médecin, which starts from the northern end of the place, away from the sea. Many people assume the street is named after the present Mayor of Nice, but he is Jacques Médecin, not Jean.

The avenue is Nice's main shopping street. Here are the **Nouvelles Galeries,** a major department store; a branch of **Prisunic,** the Gallic equivalent of Woolworth's; and the **Etoile,** a *centre commercial,* or shopping mall, with shops on several floors linked by escalators and unusual sci-fi elevators. On the top floor there is a cafeteria serving inexpensive snacks and there is also a good bookshop, the **FNAC,** with some English books and plentiful guidebooks. The avenue Thiers, which leads off to the left from the top of avenue Jean-Médecin, has the railway station, the main tourist office, and the Post Office.

The second useful avenue from the place Masséna, which leaves it to the east, the only direction not so far explored, is the avenue Félix Faure, with the gardens and fountains of the Espace Masséna on the right. About 300 yards along is the Gare Centrale TN, the town bus station, and a further 300 yards beyond that is the Gare Routière, the bus station for trips out of Nice. From here it is only a short walk to the northern end of the old town—cut down through the place St.-François or walk along the boulevard Jean-Jaures to the place Garibaldi.

If you ignore both diversions, and continue along the avenue Félix Faure, you will see that it changes its name twice. First it becomes avenue St.-Jean-Baptiste and then, just as it becomes avenue Gallieni it passes the vast convention center and exhibition hall known as the Acropolis but more properly entitled the **Palais des Arts, du Tourisme et des Congrès.** This has its own tourist office.

There are a number of other places which are well

worth a visit in and around Nice, but which entail a longer walk from the center than is comfortable. However, all are easily reached by bus, by car, or by taxi.

The **Musée Chagall** is on the boulevard de Cimiez. Take bus 15 and get off at the Docteur-Moriez stop. For those traveling by car there is an underground parking lot here. The museum was purpose-built to house the glorious Chagall collection, with windows large enough to show the pictures in the Mediterranean light in which they were painted. At the heart of the collection, which was a gift from the artist to the country where he had lived and worked for so many years, are the 17 huge and magical canvases of *The Message of the Bible*, created over a period of 13 years. There are also sculptures, a mosaic, and more than 195 preliminary sketches. In case so much culture makes you peckish, snacks, ice creams, and drinks are served in the garden. Open from 10 to 7 from July through September; other months there is a two-hour lunch break from 12:30 and an earlier closing time of 5; completely closed Tuesdays and public holidays. Note that this is the only museum in Nice to charge for admission, except on Wednesdays when entry is free.

For yet more culture, head towards Cimiez which has been the elegant residential district of Nice since Victorian times. Take one of the bus routes 15, 17, 20, or 22 to the Arènes stop. The **Musée Matisse,** 163 avenue des Arènes-de-Cimiez, is housed in a 17th-century Italian villa, itself built on the site of a Roman villa. Inside are Roman, Greek, Etruscan and other statues and remains, most of them found on the site. Upstairs are paintings by Matisse illustrating the various stages of his career, and also drawings, bronzes, and some of the artist's furniture and personal belongings. The museum is open from 10 to noon and 2:30 to 6:30 from May to September; and from 10 to noon and 2 to 5 the rest of the year. It is closed Sunday mornings, Mondays, and in November.

On the far side of the museum are the foundations of the **Roman town** and its **arena,** open the same times as the museum. Originally Cimiez was Cemenelum, a settlement which had about 20,000 inhabitants by the second century A.D. The remains are interesting but not spectacular, partly because the arena is small by Roman standards and would have held no more than 4,000 spectators. It all comes to riotous life, though, when the summer jazz festival is held here.

Nearby is the Franciscan monastery of **Notre-Dame-de-l'Assomption.** Its buildings can be seen on guided visits daily except on Saturday afternoons, Sundays, and public holidays. There is a museum and an audiovisual show setting out the beliefs and works of the Franciscan order. The monastery church has paintings by the 15th-century Niçois artists Louis and Antoine Bréa. The terraced gardens to the south of the monastery command splendid views out over Nice.

La Musée des Beaux-Arts, alias Musée Chéret, at 23 avenue des Baumettes, is not far away. It was built in 1878 as the home away from home of a Russian princess and is now an enticing art gallery with entire rooms devoted to the works of Dufy, Van Dongen, and Gustav-Adolf Mossa and with important works by Fragonard, Rubens, and Caravaggio. There are sculptures by Rodin, Carpeaux, and Volti, some Picasso ceramics, two oriental galleries, and a particularly beguiling Impressionist Gallery hung with pictures by Renoir, Degas, Monet, and Sisley. It's open from 10 to noon and 3 to 6, May through September, and 2 to 5 the rest of the year. It closes Mondays, public holidays, and November.

At the western edge of Nice, out beyond the station, is the boulevard de Tsarévitch, and here stands the **Russian Orthodox Cathedral,** magnificently exuberant beneath its six onion domes. Built mainly as a result of the generous contributions of Tsar Nicholas II, it was consecrated in 1912. The tsars are no more, but the cathedral still has worshippers, and other visitors who come to marvel at the rich interior with its delicate frescoes and sumptuous iconostasis. There are guided visits, mornings and afternoons, though on Sundays and the holy days of the Russian Orthodox Church the tours are afternoons only.

Down near the harbor, where the bustle of boats is worth a visit in its own right, is the **Musée Terra Amata,** 25 boulevard Carnot. This is a museum of local prehistory, built on the site of an excavation which uncovered the print of a human foot whose owner had walked here 400,000 years ago. Relics of one of Europe's earliest settlements are displayed, and the life-style of the people is explained in film and (English) recorded commentary. It is open from 10 to noon and 2 to 7, May to mid-September, shutting an hour earlier the rest of the year. It is always shut on Mondays, public holidays, and during the second half of September.

INFORMATION

● **Tourist Offices.** The main tourist office is by the rail station at av. Thiers (tel. 93–87–07–07). The **Accueil de France** office is here too, where hotel reservations can be made for anywhere in France, but not more than eight days in advance. All deposits are refundable, but there is a charge for telexes. Other branches are at 5 av. Gustav-V, just off the promenade des Anglais, by the Jardin Albert Ier; at the Acropolis Center; and at the airport parking lot. From any office you can pick up a good town plan, and a list of hotels and furnished flats to let.

● **Post Code.** The post code for Nice is 06000. It must be used when writing to any Nice address.

● **Car Hire. Avis,** 2 rue des Phocéens (tel. 93–80–63–52). **Europcar,** 89 rue de France (tel. 93–87–08–53). **Hertz,** 12 av. du Suede (tel. 93–81–51–21). **Interent,** Gare SNCF (tel. 93–88–00–18). All but Interent also have desks at Nice airport.

● **Boat Hire.** Boats can't be hired at Nice, you'll have to go to Antibes or Cannes. But for guided excursions, try **Gallus,** 24 quai Lunel (tel. 93–55–33–33).

● **Helicopters.** There is a spectacular—and expensive—six-minute helicopter ride from Nice airport to Monaco. Go by chopper, return by train, or, if you win at the tables, fly both ways!

ACCESS

Nice is extremely convenient to get to by air. From London the plane journey takes two hours, from New York seven and a half. The busy Nice airport is on the seafront, on an extension of the promenade des Anglais. Few international airports are so conveniently located. Buses leave there every few minutes for the center of town, a trip which takes 15 minutes. Of course, there are also taxis.

For the motorist, Nice is on the main A8 expressway, which continues east into Italy via Genoa.

There are regular bus services to Nice from many other European cities: Geneva, Madrid, and Brussels among them. For details check with the Gare Routière (tel. 93-85-61-81). For buses arriving from London, Barcelona, and Valencia check with Phocéens Car, 2 place Masséna (93-85-66-61).

Train services run regularly from Paris and other parts of France, and from all major European cities. The Motorail service (*train-auto-couchette*) allows travelers to put their car on the train in Paris and wake up in Nice. A regular car ferry also runs from Corsica.

For those who want to travel in style there's a regular helicopter service from the airport to Monte Carlo which takes 15 minutes and costs 300 frs. For details contact **Heli-Air Monaco** (tel. 93-72-34-62). **Heli-Transport,** otherwise known as Cannes-St.-Tropez Helicoptères, also has helicopter services between the airport and St.-Tropez, Cannes (Palm Beach), Fréjus, and Monte Carlo. For reservations call 93-83-69-11 (Nice airport); 93-43-11-11 (Cannes); or 94-97-36-45 (St.-Tropez).

HAPPENINGS

Nice is lively almost all the year round, although November and the first half of December are a little quiet and the weather can be less than cheerful. But in early spring the famous Carnival fills the extravagantly decorated streets and squares with excited crowds for a fortnight. The carnival atmosphere is alive from the processional entry of King Carnival, attended by floats and outriders in picturesque and sometimes grotesque costumes, until his ceremonial burning on Mardi Gras (Shrove Tuesday) itself. Throughout King Carnival's brief but glorious reign there are flower battles, fireworks, processions, masked balls, and enough ebullience to drive the gloom of winter away for at least ten months.

March brings an international fair to the Acropolis Center, the end of the Paris to Nice cycle race, and a marathon. April has the Nice International Tennis Tournament. In July the great Jazz Parade draws in more than 300 jazz musicians from all over the world for a ten-day session in the Cimiez Arena, every day from 5 to midnight.

In August there are more flower battles, along the promenade, and glittering firework displays, as well as a wine festival in the Cimiez Gardens. September is a little more serious by comparison, with the start of the big-game fishing season and other sporting events. In October culture takes over and holds sway until May with a season of opera and symphony concerts in the grand Opera House.

Other major shows are staged throughout the year in the new theater at the Acropolis which, with its seating capacity of 2,500 and its 12,900 square feet of stage, is second only in France to the Paris Opera House.

LODGING

Meridien (L), 1 promenade des Anglais (tel. 93–82–25–25). 297 rooms. Open all year. Nice has three hotels in the (L) class, and this is one of them. It is superbly run, modern, and conveniently located—but anyone willing to pay top prices should consider staying at the unique Negresco.

Negresco (L), 37 promenade des Anglais (tel. 93–88–39–51). 140 rooms. Open all year, though sometimes closed in November for improvements. Opened by a Romanian, Henri Negresco, in 1912, in the presence of eight kings, the hotel is renowned for its elegance and luxury. The centerpiece of the vast marble-floored, glass-domed salon is a crystal chandelier which weighs a ton. The circular Aubusson carpet—the biggest in the world, naturally—cost 560,000 gold frs. when it was laid. The hotel was lavishly patronized by the rich and famous for two years, and then came the Great War when it was commandeered as a hospital. By the time Jeanne and Paul Augier bought it in 1957 it was a shadow of its former glittering self. Madame Augier initiated a massive restoration, visiting châteaux to acquire entire antique coffered ceilings and magnificent fireplaces for the public rooms. No two bedrooms are alike and each has genuine antique furniture and good pictures to complement its individual decor.

If you can afford to stay, ask to see as many of the rooms as possible; if you can't, then at least call in for a drink at the bar, or a cup of tea or coffee. Since 1974 the Negresco has been classified as an historical monument, and it shouldn't be missed.

Jacques Maximin, the young chef, is now almost as famous as the hotel itself, (see *Restaurant* listings). Of the two restaurants the **Chantecler** is the more expensive, while **La Rotonde** is less formal in style and price.

La Pérouse (E), 11 quai Rauba-Capeu (tel. 93–62–34–63). 63 rooms. Open all year. Located at the foot of the Castle Hill, between the old town quarter and the port. *Rauba Capeu* is Provençal for "hat robber," and at times the wind can be brisk, but the view makes it all worthwhile. Each of the splendid rooms has a balcony or terrace overlooking the sea (the road is busy, but the sound-proofing is effective). A heated swimming pool appeals to those who wish to avoid the shingly beach.

Pullman (E), 28 av. Notre Dame (tel. 93–80–30–24). 200 rooms with air-conditioning. Open all year. It's located just off the av. Jean Médecin, towards the station end, with the promenade a good ten-minute walk away. The hotel was called the Frantel until the spring of 1987 and there is still occasional confusion between the old and new names. A comfortable place to stay with a swimming pool on the roof, and an underground parking lot.

Sofitel-Splendid (E), 50 blvd. Victor Hugo (tel. 93–88–69–54). 116 rooms. Open all year. This one is centrally located, four blocks back from the promenade des Anglais down rue Meyerbeer. There's a swimming pool on the 8th floor (the roof) with great views out over town. The Sofitel-Splendid is the happiest kind of marriage between tradition and modernity—it is an old hotel, reconstructed along modern lines, but maintaining all the elegant integrity it had before.

Victoria (M), 33 blvd. Victor Hugo (tel. 93–88–39–60). 39 rooms. Open all year. Here is the old-world charm you'd expect of a hotel called Victoria. All the rooms are well-appointed, but the best are the ones overlooking the pleasant garden. It has no restaurant, but the **Bistrot d'Antoine** (see *Restaurants*) is opposite and there are plenty of other places to eat nearby.

Durante (I), 16 av. Durante (tel. 93–88–84–40). 26 rooms. Closed November and first week in December. On a rather dull street near the station, where many of Nice's inexpensive hotels cluster, but worth recommending because the more expensive rooms have kitchenettes —as well as TV, private bath and toilet—which makes it possible to keep down the cost of eating. It is also a very convenient base for train excursions to other parts of the Riviera.

Gourmet Lorrain (I), 17 av. Santa-Fio (tel. 93–84–90–78). 15 rooms, a few with bath and air-conditioning.

Open all year. It's two miles from the place Masséna, so is more suitable for those with cars than those without. Although it's best known for its restaurant (*see below*), it's also a quiet, inexpensive place to stay.

Suisse (I), 15 quai Rauba-Capeu (tel. 92–62–33–00). 40 rooms. Open all year. Tunis is near La Perouse and is a cheaper base from which to enjoy the same good views.

Lodging Information
There should never be a problem finding accommodation in Nice since it has 9,852 hotel rooms. The tourist office has a complete list of all hotels, with full details, and will send it abroad to you if you enclose an international reply coupon with the request. The tourist office grades the hotels, using a star-system (which has nothing to do with Michelin stars) that goes from one to four. In general the three- and four-star hotels fit into the (L) or (E) categories of this guide. Two-star hotels can generally offer private bath, shower or toilet, and many hotels in the one-star category also have them. All hotels should exhibit their official stars and prices outside—if they don't, the information should be in the lobby.

DINING

Ane Rouge (E), 7 quai Deux-Emmanuel (tel. 93–89–49–63). Open Monday to Friday, closed public holidays and mid-July through September. This is a serious restaurant, located right on the port, where the owners—the Vidalots—devote themselves to satisfying the discerning local diners. Tourists are welcome, but the restaurant doesn't exist primarily for them. Some of Nice's best seafood is served here. Note the closing dates.

Chantecler (E). This is the Negresco's main restaurant. Details as for the hotel, except that the restaurant always closes November. This is without doubt the best restaurant in Nice and, indeed, one of the top in the world. Foodie literature refers constantly to the chef, Jacques Maximin, with a surfeit of adjectives. In fact, it *is* hard to write objectively about his food—all one can safely say is that there is universal agreement as to its stupendously high quality, as one would expect from one of the leading advocates of *nouvelle cuisine*. You'll probably have to take out a second mortgage to eat here, but it would be worth it!

Coco Beach (E), 2 avenue Jean-Lorrain (tel. 93-89-39-26). Closed Sundays, Mondays, and mid-November to mid-December. Drive a mile east of the port to find this restaurant, where well-heeled tourists tuck into fresh grilled fish and lobsters in front of a dramatic view of the bay.

Albert's Bar (M), 1 rue M. Jaubert (tel. 93-53-37-72). Open Monday to Saturday, closed public holidays and first half of August. This is charmingly old-fashioned in decor and atmosphere. Try the salad and mixed grill for a satisfying and unpretentious meal.

Barale (M), 39 rue Beaumont (tel. 93-89-17-94). Open Tuesday to Saturday, closed August. Barale is run by a remarkable woman who, if she is in the mood, will sing to you, and perhaps make you sing too. It is essential to reserve before 10 A.M. on the day. There is only one menu—you have what you're told to have!—but that's fine because the food is Niçois and very good. Aperitifs, wine, and service are all included in the price. Perhaps not everybody's cup of *bouillabaisse,* but for those who enjoy a slightly bizarre experience it's well worth trying.

Les Dents de la Mer (M), 2 rue St.-François-de-Paule (tel. 93-80-99-16). Always open. This was the French title for the film *Jaws,* and the decor inside is unashamedly kitsch. It looks like a tourist trap, but is, in fact, a fine seafood restaurant, and very popular with the local people.

Florian (M), 22 rue Alphonse-Karr (tel. 93-88-86-60). Closed Sundays, Monday lunch, and early June to late August. You'll find excellent food and service here in a calm and sedate atmosphere. The restaurant is sited in the heart of town, just off boulevard Victor Hugo.

La Rotonde (M), in the Negresco. Open all the year round, and every day until midnight. Wonderfully uninhibited decor, with a carousel motif, and a cheerful atmosphere. Simpler, and cheaper, versions of the great chef Maximin's food are served here. It's very good value and almost at the (I) level, if you're not too greedy.

Le Bistrot d'Antoine (I), 26 blvd. Victor-Hugo (tel. 93-88-49-75). Open Monday to Saturday. Delicious fare, delicately cooked by Antoine Villa, and very good value. The decor is ultra-refined—blushingly pink—and all the paintings on the walls are for sale.

Le Gourmet Lorrain (I), 7 av. Santa-Fior (tel. 93-84-90-78). Open Tuesday to Saturday, closed August and first half of January. This is the restaurant of the hotel of the same name (the hotel is always open). It's two miles from the center, but is well worth making the journey for the sake of the food. There is an enormous wine cellar, holding 50,000 bottles, and if you get carried away and order something special the check could slip into the (M) category. The best of the menu are the traditional French dishes for which the patron—Alain Leloup—is justly famous.

La Merande (I), 4 rue Terrasse, in the old town. Closed Saturday evenings, Sundays, Mondays, and February and August. Monsieur Giusti refuses to have a telephone, so reservations are impossible. Go early and be prepared to find there's no room left because the good honest local food is so deservedly popular. Try pasta with *pistou*, authentic stockfish, succulent tripe, and *ratatouille*.

La Petite Maison Ferrier (I) and (M), corner of rue de l'Opéra and rue St.-François-de-Paule (tel. 93-92-59-59). Open Monday to Saturday. This is conveniently located between the place Masséna and the old town. It's very popular and can be crowded, so reservations are a good idea. The food is excellent, and includes very imaginative dishes and good desserts.

Le Grand Café de Turin (I), place Garibaldi. Open daily from 8. This is in a class of its own. The interior looks rather seedy, like a pre-war café with fly-blown notices about *Répression de l'Ivresse Publique*. The clientele is a classless mix of tourists, eminent executives, housewives taking a break from shopping, and elderly men holding forth over a glass of red wine. In season the great attraction is the oyster shop, outside, where the shells are opened while you watch and are served with brown bread, pats of butter and perhaps a jug of cool white

Muscadet. For this experience you pay only 20 percent more than if you had bought oysters to take home, and considerably less than if you had ordered them in a smart restaurant. If shellfish are not enough—or sadly out of season—go round the corner to the *socca* stall. *Socca* is a heavy eggless pancake, a yard in diameter. It's made of chick pea flour, and needs plenty of salt and pepper. It costs a few pence a portion and the *socca* merchant will lend you a plate which you can leave at the café when you've finished with it.

NIGHTCLUBS

Camargue, 6 pl. Charles-Félix, on the cours Saleya (tel. 93–85–74–10). This is the best but you have to get past the doorman first.

Escurial, 29 rue Alphonse Karr. This is a much bigger disco, with elaborate lighting effects, and the occasional live show.

Findlatter's, 6 rue Léponte. Most nights this one is full of well-heeled students—French yuppies-to-be. The food is superior to the usual disco fare.

Ruhl Casino, promenade des Anglais (tel. 93–87–95–87). This re-opened in 1987 after years of libelous rumors of skulduggery. Even if you don't play, it's worth going in to watch the rest of the clientele, mesmerized by the turn of the wheel.

Sinclair, 4 rue Masséna. Drag's the gear here. You don't *have* to wear it, and if the sight of it *en masse* worries you, then you should try elsewhere.

SHOPPING

For elegant, expensive shopping it might be best to take a trip to Cannes or Monaco. For everything-under-one-roof there are the **Nouvelles Galeries** and the **Etoile** in the av. Jean-Médecin (see *Exploring*).

For food, whether for self-caterers or for those wanting to take home edible souvenirs and presents, Nice is an excellent hunting ground. Gourmet shrines include **Auer,** 7 rue St.-François-de-Paule, home of the best crystallized fruits in the world. They are expensive but unique and sold nowhere else. (The ice creams and pastries are exceptional, too). **Alziari** at 14 rue St.-François-de-Paule, nearly opposite, is a tiny shop with a big reputation. Many people swear that M. Alziari's olive oil is the best anywhere—the locals take it away by the gallon, literally. Visitors can buy cans with old-fashioned labels, or Provençal herbs and spices. For pastries, don't miss **Vogade,** 1 pl. Masséna. Your souvenir from here will be the memory of airy lightness and delicate flavors—and probably an inch round the waist!

Self-caterers should visit the **street market,** Cours Saleya, in the Old Town, Mondays 7:30 to 5:30. This is the street for all kinds of provisions; every day, **Agu,** the master butcher, is here, too. For cheese, outside market days, the best place is **La Ferme Fromagère,** 13 rue Assalit. Those who prefer superior ready-made dishes should seek out **Callaud,** 2 rue Maccarani, off the rue Masséna.

For reading matter—in French or English—try **Actuel,** 28 rue Masséna, which stays open till late.

One place not to miss is **Cap 3000,** a huge shopping mall with dozens of boutiques, a department store, and a supermarket. It's at St.-Laurent-du-Var, about five minutes' drive west from Nice airport, and makes a very interesting comparison with the shopping malls back home.

Excursions

The alps by train

Nice is the most convenient center on the Riviera for public transport. Frequent trains run along the coast, and any of the places between St.-Raphael and Ventimiglia can be visited in a day or even half a day. A few trains take a more dramatic route, heading slowly up the

Alps to Cuneo in Italy, via the tunnel at the Col de Tende, stopping along the way at enchanting mountain villages. Details from tourist offices or the station: Gare SNCF, av. Thiers (tel. 93-87-50-50); special post code 06049 Nice Cedex.

DIGNE

Another trip through lovely scenery is on the delightful narrow gauge railroad that runs 90 miles inland to **Digne,** an attractive little spa town. The route wanders north and then west, taking in **Annot** and other stops on the way, and makes a perfect day's outing, through some of the most attractive scenery of the Alps foothills. There are four trains a day in each direction, and the trip averages around three hours. The station for this service is the Gare de Provence, 33 av. Malusséna (tel. 93-84-89-71).

SKIING

This is not a sport usually connected with the Riviera, but in fact Nice is a major starting point for some very fine ski slopes. **Auron** is 60 miles away and has pistes of all levels of difficulty, plus 25 ski lifts, 80 instructors, and first class hotels. **Valberg** and **Isola 2000** are two other top class ski resorts; both of them nearer to Nice. Closer still are a number of lesser places with ski lifts but few other facilities. For information write to **Ski Azur,** CRT, 55 Promenade des Anglais, 06000 Nice, or to the tourist office.

OTHER DAY TRIPS

As well as its accessibility as a rail nexus, Nice is the center of a dense network of regular services by bus and boat, many with English-speaking guides. Details are readily available from the tourist offices.

From Nice to Monaco and Menton

Menton lies beyond Monaco. It is practical to describe in a single section the roads linking Nice to both places. For simplicity, they are described from west to east, from the driver's point of view. Places on the *basse corniche* road can be reached by train; others by bus. Most excursions take the form of going out by one road and returning by another. There are four roads:

—**La Basse Corniche** (N98 or *corniche inférieure*). This runs along the coast, and is a delight for passengers—who can admire the glorious Riviera views—but grim for drivers who see little but heavy traffic. There are plenty of pleasant places to stop en route, but impatient or nervous drivers should probably take one of the other roads.

If you do go this way, the first stop is **Villefranche.** Park near the port, which is charming and plentifully supplied with cafés. The bay here, between Nice and the Peninsula, lies in the crater of a submerged and extinct volcano, and is deep enough for fleets of warships to anchor safely. Ramble in the old town, around the **Eglise St.-Michel,** and then return to the car and drive round the **St.-Jean-Cap-Ferrat** peninsula with its luscious vegetation and wealthy inhabitants. Visit the **Foundation Rothschild**—a fine Italianate house, with an extensive collection of works of art, set in 17 acres of superb gardens. Guided visits are available afternoons only, and it is closed Mondays and in November. When the house is closed you can still walk around the gardens, open every morning except Sundays.

Beaulieu is the next place worth stopping at. It sometimes is called *Petite Afrique* (Little Africa), presumably because of the magnificent palm trees that lend an exotic air to the place. It was once one of the leaders of the social pack on the Riviera, and still guards an aura of distant elegance. A walk along the promenade Maurice-Rouvier which follows the shoreline towards St.-Jean-Cap-Ferrat, will tell you a lot about the way things used to be in the great turn-of-the-century. Needless to say, men must wear ties to visit the Beaulieu casino, 8 av. Blundell Maple (tel. 93–01–00–39).

On a promontory overlooking the Baie des Fourmis, is the **Villa Kérylos,** a magnificently reconstructed classical Greek villa, built by an archeologist in the first decade of the century and left to the nation in 1928. It's open for rather odd hours: 3 to 7 on summer afternoons (July and August); 2 to 6 the rest of the year; closed November and Mondays.

For a relaxed lunch, try the **African Queen** (M) on the harbor (tel. 93–01–10–85). For a more splendid spread, with quite exceptional seafood, you should visit the restaurant of **La Métropole** (E), blvd. Maréchal-Leclerc (tel. 93–01–00–08). The restaurant has a big terrace with terrific views out over the sea.

A few miles farther on is Monaco, which has a chapter of its own, and just beyond lies **Roquebrune-Cap-Martin.** To get the feel of this engaging hilltop village you should spend at least an hour struggling up and down the steps of its narrow streets. Two 500-year-old processions are held here on Good Friday and August 5, when the villagers perform a mini-Oberammergau, with colorful costumes and medieval tradition. When you have soaked up the atmosphere, take the road to the point of the cape, av. Winston Churchill, park by the footpath signposted **promenade le Corbusier** and decide if you can spare an hour and a half to walk all the way to Monte Carlo (and back again, to pick up the car). Drive on and the next stop is Menton, which also has its own chapter.

—**La Moyenne Corniche** (N7). This is a much wider road which avoids built-up areas and offers splendid views. The road climbs up to the Col de Villefranche, which looks down on the bay of Villefranche and Cap Ferrat. After negotiating the tunnel, take the narrow D34 to the parking lot on the **Plateau-St.-Martin.** Here a *table d'orientation,* 1,200 feet above sea level, helps to identify the various places you can see. Continue to **Eze** and turn off the N7 to examine this eagle's nest of a village. Although it is a little touristy, the **Jardin Exotique,** open mornings and afternoons, is a must; on a fine morning you can see as far as Corsica. The N7 road stays in French territory above Monaco, but a zigzag road wriggles down from it to Monte Carlo. Staying on the N7, join the *basse corniche* just before Roquebrune.

—**La Grande Corniche** (D2564) is the earliest of these four roads. Before Napoleon built it nothing but mule tracks crossed this way, and most travelers went from Nice to Genoa by sea. On a fine day it offers superb views, made magical at night by the Riviera lights. Make a stop at the **Belvédère d'Eze** for views in both directions, of the coast and of the Alps. Leave the main road at the pretty village of **La Turbie,** 1,500 feet above sea level, to admire **La Trophée des Alpes,** the remnants of a Roman monument erected to the glory of Augustus Caesar. Go past the road which leads down to Monaco and make a further stop at **La Vistaëro** for one more glorious view before the *grande corniche* descends to sea level at Roquebrune.

—**The A8 Expressway.** Anyone driving from the west, wanting neither to stop in Nice nor to take any of the much slower corniche roads, should get onto the expressway. This remarkable feat of engineering sweeps around the north of Nice and heads on into Italy, through tunnels and over viaducts, with exits for Monaco and Menton on the way. Be aware of signposting here: in French, Genoa (which is the direction eastwards as you leave Nice) is "Gênes" and Ventimiglia is "Vintimille." If you go on into Italy for an excursion, note that Genoa then becomes "Genova" and Nice becomes "Nizza."

Monaco

The principality of Monaco has the shortest coastline of any sovereign state. Its entire land area measures just under one square mile, squeezed between the Alpes Maritimes on one side and the sea on the other; only the Vatican City is smaller. It's not surprising, then, that the land is being artificially extended into the sea, that an important hotel complex paddles out into the water on piles, and that many of the modern buildings tower skywards.

The country divides neatly into four quarters. The picturesque old town, where the Palace stands in its beautiful grounds, is built on a rocky promontory, **le Rocher.** To the other side of the Port de Monaco lies the resort of **Monte Carlo,** still synonymous with gambling and glamor. Between them is the commercial and residential area of **La Condamine.** Tucked down behind the old town is **Fontvieille** where industry flourishes discreetly on reclaimed land.

Despite the fact that it is a sovereign state, Monaco has no obvious frontier. There is no passport control, no customs shed, not even a symbolic barrier. The coinage and stamps, the uniforms of the ubiquitous police and the fancy dress of the tiny army are all Monegasque, but the language, food, and way of life are French. To an unobservant visitor it might at first appear to be just another smallish French town—with a population of only 28,500 while Nice has 338,500. But Monaco has its own atmosphere, and it's a rich one. There's so much money here that you can almost smell it. There are numerous banks, consulates of all nations, extravagant buildings—and, although these days only four percent of the state revenue comes from the gaming tables and slot machines, tourism is still exceedingly important. Callers at the tourist office are sent tottering out with armfuls of lavishly produced free tourist literature to ensure that they miss none of the extravagant delights.

It wasn't always like this. Before the 1860s the stony little principality was broke—so much so that the Grimaldi prince of those days, Charles III, sold Menton and Roquebrune to France. Then gaming turned the tables. At that time gambling was forbidden in France, but casinos had been opened in two German states, Baden-Baden and Bad Homburg, and rich foreigners were lining up to be parted from their wealth; an irresistible challenge.

First, a modest casino was opened in the old town of Monaco. Later a company, decorously entitled the Société des Bains de Mer, "the Sea Bathing Company," was set up, and a large casino was built on an unpromising piece of goat pasture a short way along the coast. At first it was a depressing failure. Millionaires were understandably reluctant to make the four-hour overland trip from Nice to Monaco by mule, or to entrust themselves to an open boat for an hour and a half. Then the new railway brought economic salvation. Once the journey was quick and comfortable, the rich were happy to undertake it, and the casino began to make a fortune. Real estate boomed, luxury hotels and an opera house were built, and a cathedral rose from the ruins of St. Nicolas' church. The hill on which the wonder-working casino stood was renamed Mount Charles—Monte Carlo—after the sovereign. Gradually the small town grew to resemble the fashionable center of a capital city.

At first the citizens of neighboring Nice were peeved. They complained that the casino was offering them unfair competition and threatened to march on Monte Carlo unless it was closed down. They got their way—but were disconcerted to find that without the lure of the nearby gaming tables business dropped off dramatically in their own hotels. Within a few months they were petitioning for the roulette wheels to start spinning again.

Nowadays, of course, there are plenty of casinos in France and Italy, and Monte Carlo's own is no longer the main attraction here. What Monaco now has to offer is a luxurious infrastructure, a unique mix of European suavity and American know-how, old-world charm blended skilfully with slick modernization. The Société des Bains de Mer still runs the casino, but also manages some of the world's best hotels. The first-class leisure facilities include an expertly-created artificial beach, and outstanding entertainment from grand opera to night-club cabaret. Conventions and conferences are hosted with style, and the flow of visitors continues throughout the year.

There are several ways to enjoy Monaco—but gambling doesn't have to be one of them. The casino doesn't figure hugely in Monaco's present life, and those who find it boring or expensive need not fret that they've missed an essential piece of local color.

If you're on a tight budget, a day trip by train allows time to get the feel of the place. It's true that there are some inexpensive hotels, but Monaco is not really designed for economic life-styles; they can be lived more successfully in Nice or Menton.

If you do have money to spare, there's plenty to spend it on: sumptuous hotels, gourmet restaurants, astonishingly varied nightlife, all attended by the smoothest and most charming of service. The ravages of high living can be repaired, up to a point, by spa beauty treatments (an effervescent seaweed bath will run away with 100 frs. in a half hour). If a week's stay is a possibility, note that there are various package deals available—for example with the Monaco golf club which is, necessarily, over the border in France.

But the best way to experience Monaco is to splash out on one night at a top hotel, perhaps the Hôtel de

Paris or Loews, and sample what the tourist literature calls "a dream come true" in this extraordinary mini-world.

Exploring

Although small in area, Monaco is long and narrow in shape and built on such a craggy outcrop that the mile between the old town and Monte Carlo seems a long way, with an inordinate number of ups and downs. For this reason it is worth taking taxis or using the town bus service. (There is a flat rate for bus journeys, whatever the distance. A book of eight tickets saves 50 percent, and is a wise buy if you plan four or more journeys.) There are also public elevators, strategically placed on the most demanding of the inclines. Bus routes, parking lots, and elevators are all listed in the tourist office leaflet *Getting About the Principality*.

The place du Casino is the centre of Monte Carlo, and even if gambling is not on your agenda you shouldn't ignore the **Casino** entirely. It is open daily, except on May 1, from 10 to 4 the following morning. No one under 21 is allowed in and passport or identity card must be produced at the door. The oldest part of the building is by Garnier, architect of the Paris Opera House, and is as elaborately ornate as anyone could wish. There are stupendous sea views from the terrace but the main activity is in the American room where the one-armed bandits clunk away from 10 in the morning. There is an admission charge for the public gaming rooms and a higher charge to look in on the private, or club, rooms, which is where the smart set play. It may not be quite what it was, but it is still impressive in its way, and conveys a taste of those extravagant *fin de siècle* days which now seem more like an operetta than real life.

Next door to the Casino are the **Hôtel de Paris** and **Loews,** (see *Hotels*), two of the best in Europe. Go in for a cup of coffee and sink into extravagant luxury, especial-

109   MONACO

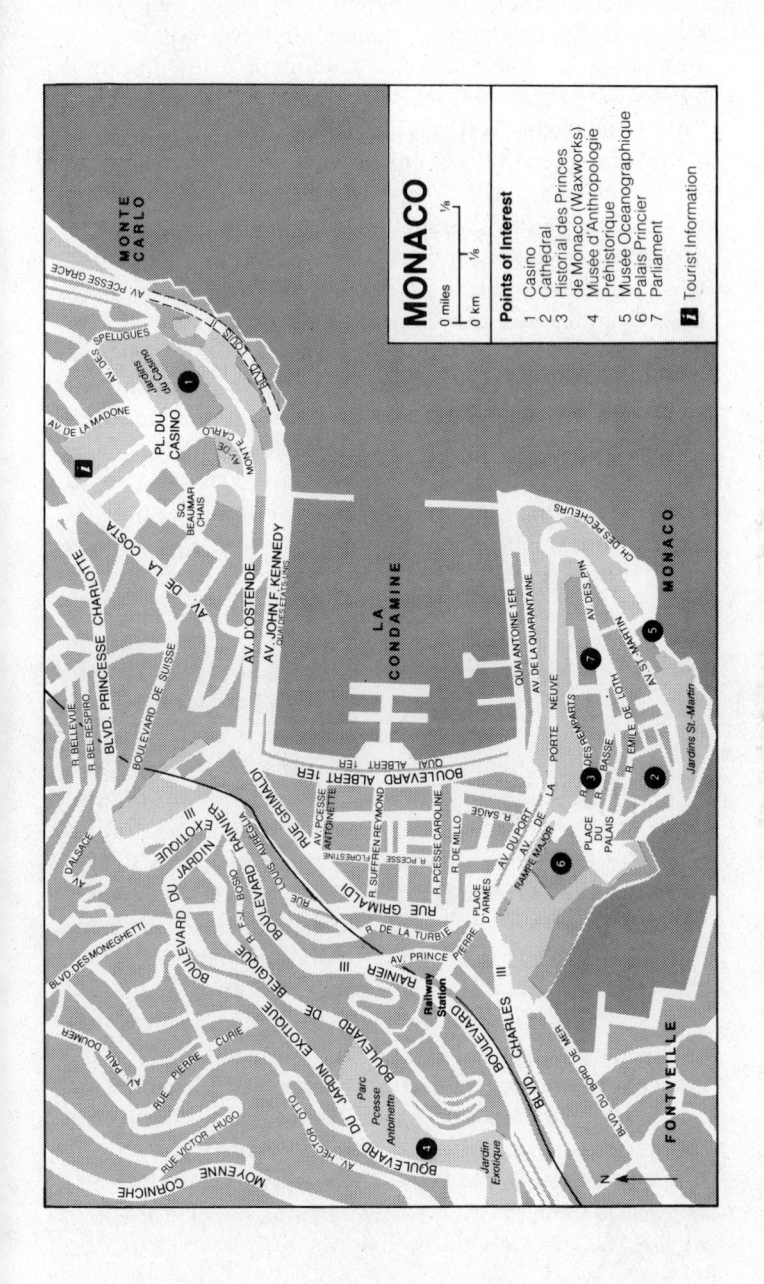

ly in the former, or a flutter in the latter's casino (which has largely taken over from its stately ancestor).

Uphill, through the pleasant terraced gardens of the Casino, is the boulevard Moulins, where you will find the tourist office. The place des Moulins is a few hundred yards along the boulevard, and from here an elevator will take you to the **National Museum** and the **Larvotto Beach** complex in the avenue Princess Grace. Housed in a Garnier villa, set in an appealing garden, the museum has a strange and compelling collection of 18th- and 19th-century dolls, and of automata who go through their paces several times a day and shamelessly show off their complex inner workings. It is open from 10 to 12:15 and 2:30 to 6:30 daily, except for some public holidays.

In the old town—Monaco Ville on its rock—the key sight is the **Prince's Palace,** a grandiose Italianate structure with a Moorish tower. The Grimaldi dynasty has ruled here since 1297, and Prince Rainier III still lives in the Palace, which is why it is only open to the public at certain times. The Changing of the Guard, though, is a daily spectacle at 11:55. Guided tours are led around inside the Palace from July to mid-October, between 9:30 and 6:30. The visits take in the ornate state apartments, and the wing which contains the **Museum of Napoleonic Souvenirs** and the **Palace Archives.** The souvenirs of Napoleon include some personal effects and, upstairs, the collection spelling out the history of Monaco also displays a sample of moon rock, for no apparent reason.

A stroll through the narrow medieval streets of the old town leads to what some call the Principality's chief attraction, the **Oceonography Museum and Aquarium,** which is also an internationally important research institution. Albert I (1848–1922), son of Charles III and great-grandfather of Prince Rainier, was an eminent and energetic marine biologist who founded the institute. The present director is the well-known underwater explorer and film maker Jacques Cousteau. There are 60 scientists on the staff using the laboratories, the two exploration ships, and the major scientific library. The museum is interesting, but the aquarium in the basement is, as it were, the high spot. An astonishing collection of the world's fish and crustacea live out their lives in public here, some of them vivid, some of them drab, a few of them the stuff of which nightmares are made. On the floors above are a wealth of whale skeletons, sea shells, and diving equipment. Take the elevator to the roof terrace for a fine view of the sea, which may look a little different now you know more about what lives in it, and a restorative drink at the bar. The museum and aquarium are open from 9:30 to 7 daily, and from 9 to 9 in July and August.

For your next surreal experience, take a bus or taxi to the **Tropical Gardens,** where 600 varieties of cacti and succulents cling to the rock face, their improbable shapes and sometimes violent coloring a further testimony to the fact that Nature will try anything once. The gardens are open from 9 to 7, or until dusk in winter; closed May 1 and November 19. Your ticket also allows you to visit the caves which open off the gardens—where some of the stalactites and stalagmites seem to imitate the shapes growing in the sunlight outside—and to go into the **Museum of Prehistoric Anthropology,** beside the gardens. The collections here trace the successive waves of humans and animals, many now extinct, that have lived in the area—with exhibits that range from primitive Stone Age tools to delicate Roman jewelry, and from the remains of mammoths to more familiar reindeer antlers.

Return to the avenue Princess Grace to discover the **plage du Larvotto,** a sweep of artificial beach, made of compressed sand. If bathing in the Mediterranean doesn't appeal, make your way to the avenue de Monte Carlo, beside the Casino, to find another of the Société des Bains de Mer's many establishments. Here there is a pool of heated sea water to swim in and all sorts of other refinements such as a sauna, a gym, a beauty salon, and a restaurant serving low calorie meals and providing a good view of the yacht harbor. Expensive, naturally—this, after all, is where the beautiful people attempt to hold on to their beauty.

INFORMATION

- **Tourist Offices.** The tourist office is at 2a blvd. des Moulins (tel. 93–30–87–01). Tourism is big business in Monaco, and the office distributes exceptionally useful, well-produced booklets and leaflets in English detailing hotels, restaurants, sports, leisure facilities, places of interest, and major events. All are informative and up to date.
- **Post Code.** The postal address of the Monaco tourist office is Direction du Tourisme, 2a blvd. des Moulins, MC 98030 MONACO. Usually, however, when writing to a Monaco address use the post code MC 98000 MONACO. Telephonically, Monaco is in France.
- **Car Hire. Avis,** 9 av. d'Oostende (tel. 93–30–17–53). **Europcar,** 47 av. de Grande-Bretagne (tel. 93–50–74–95). **Hertz,** 57 rue Grimaldi (tel. 93–50–79–60).
- **Boat Hire. Agency Boat Charter,** 17 blvd. Albert 1er (tel. 93–50–61–55), with or without crew, for tuna fishing. **Monaco Shipchandler,** 9 av. Président Kennedy (tel. 93–50–60–42).

ACCESS

For those splashing out there are daily helicopter flights from Nice airport to Monaco. The journey takes six or seven minutes, and there are shuttle links from the heliport to hotels. Also from Nice airport is a minibus service, stopping at various points in Monaco. The bus takes about 50 minutes, taxis about 40 minutes.

Motorists driving to Monaco should consult the *In Between Nice and Monaco and Menton* section (see *Nice* chapter). If coming by the A8 expressway from Nice and the west, take the Monaco-Roquebrune exit; from Italy, take the Monaco-La Turbie exit.

All trains stop at the Monaco/Monte Carlo station. The harbor has moorings for 550 vessels, up to 150 meters long. For details check the *Guide to the Port* from the tourist office, or the **Service de la Marine,** 7 av. Président Kennedy, B.P. 468, MC 98012 MONACO.

Happenings

Monaco has no off season. Restaurant staff may take a vacation now and again, but the hotels and the Casino are always open. In January the highlight is the finale of the Monte Carlo rally, when drivers emerge from the ice, snow and fog of northern Europe into Mediterranean sunshine. January 27 is a public holiday in honor of Sainte Dévote, patron saint of the Principality, and everyone takes time off for the torchlight processions and fireworks.

In February there is the International Television Festival. April sees the start of the International Open tennis championships, and also the spring music and ballet festival. In May the streets are closed for the Monte Carlo Auto Grand Prix, and in June the Monte Carlo Open golf tournament is held on the slopes of Mont Agel which, strictly speaking, is in France.

In July there is a series of open-air concerts in the courtyard of the Prince's Palace and the first of many evenings devoted to the International Fireworks Festival. The Firework Festival goes on into August with pyrotechnicians from all over the world showing off their latest bangs, flashes, and whistles. Also in August is the Red Cross Gala, held in the Sporting Club, and every two years there is an international antique dealers' and jewelers' exhibition.

There is another public holiday on Prince Rainier's birthday, November 19, which is celebrated with fireworks, dances, and a gala performance at the Opera House. December is the time for the International Circus Festival, launched by Prince Rainier in 1974, at which performers strive for gold clowns, the circus world's equivalent of oscars.

Specific details of all events are published in leaflets available from the tourist offices.

LODGING

Loews (L), av. des Spelugues (tel. 93–50–65–00). 573 rooms, 68 suites. Open all year. This is the big one, bright and modern, built on stilts out over the shore. If one day a luxury complex is built under a pressurized dome on another planet for tired space executives to relax in, then Loews will have the know-how. There are those who have been heard to mutter about brash vulgarity, but many love the place, and it certainly has everything—even a shopping mall. There are no less than five restaurants, where nonresidents are welcome, each with its own character. **Le Foie Gras** is small and luxurious, with gourmet cuisine. The **Argentin** specializes in grills, and flies its meat in from Scotland. The **Folie Russe** has a spectacular cabaret, and caviar seems to come with everything. All are (E), but it's possible to drop down to (M) level at **Le Pistou,** up on the roof terrace, which serves genuine but unalarming Provençal food. The **Café de la Mer** is an informal brasserie.

There is, of course, a swimming pool on the roof, complete with health spa and gym, each with attendants and instructors. And, naturally, there is what many regard as the specialty of the Principality—a big casino with American games and serried ranks of one-armed bandits clonking and whirring continuously as Sheiks of Araby, local housewives, and Californian yuppies feed them with 5 and 10 fr. coins and occasionally gather up a shower of winnings.

Hôtel de Paris (L), place du Casino (tel. 93–50–80–80). 206 rooms, 40 suites. Open all year. This is quite a different kettle of lobsters; here are elegance, luxury, dignity, and old-world charm. Built by the Société des Bains de Mer in 1864, it has been enlarged and modernized since, but still breathes the deep-carpeted, gold-plated splendor of an era when kings and granddukes enjoyed smooth efficient service within its walls.

There are two restaurants: the sumptuous **Louis**

XV, which, in 1987 succeeded in luring the talented chef Alain Ducasse away from the Juana at Juan-les-Pins, and the **Grill,** where on suitable nights the roof glides aside to allow diners to eat under the stars. Serving both restaurants are cellars carved out of the rock in 1874, where nearly a quarter of a million bottles of wine mature in the cool darkness. The famous bar, with its impressive entrance hall and attendant boutiques, is a good place to go at teatime or the cocktail hour. The hard up visitor, if decently clad, should take a morning Coke at Loews and afternoon tea at the Hôtel de Paris.

Alexandra (M), 35 blvd. Princesse Charlotte (tel. 93–50–63–13). 55 rooms. Open all year. This hotel is one of the few that falls into the (M) range in Monaco; it also has a few (I) rooms, none with bath or shower. It is conveniently placed close to the place du Casino.

Balmoral (M), 12 av. Costa (tel. 93–50–62–37). 68 rooms. Open all year. A very centrally sited hotel, with views over the port. Some rooms verge on the (E) grade.

Alternatives
Monaco is not well endowed with inexpensive hotels. Vacationers with economy in mind should stay in Menton or Nice and travel in daily by bus or train. A car is not much fun here—driving in the steep streets is wearisome and parking is expensive.

DINING

Bec Rouge (E), av. de Grande-Bretagne (tel. 93–30–74–91). Open all year, except January and mid-June. A quietly chic eatery where all the best Monegasques—even *the* best—are seen. The superb fish and generally traditional cooking commands fairly stiff prices.

Coupole (M) to (E), 1 av. Princesse Grace (tel. 93–25–45–45). Open daily, but closed for lunch from late June to early September. This is the restaurant at the Mirabeau hotel, another Société des Bains de Mer establishment, and has impeccable standards of both food and service.

Dominique le Stanc (E), 18 blvd. des Moulins (tel. 93-50-63-37). Open Tuesday to Saturday. Some authorities cite this as Monaco's best restaurant. The delicate and inventive cuisine doesn't fall back on the obvious *foie gras*, caviar, and lobster to justify high prices. It is only small, so reservations are essential in high season.

Louis XV (E), Hôtel de Paris. This is a serious contender for top restaurant in Monaco. The food is wonderful, and the decor is worth a visit in its own right. But if you are after a really trendy restaurant, try the modern 8th floor Grill, with its magnificent view and sliding roof.

Restaurant du Port (M), quai Albert Ier (tel. 95-50-67-94). Open Wednesday to Monday, closed November. Excellent Italian cuisine with particularly good fish dishes. The terrace has a good view of the harbor and those small liners that tycoons refer to as yachts.

Polpetta (I), rue Paradis (tel. 93-50-67-94). Open Wednesday to Monday, closed February. This popular Italian restaurant is close enough to the Italian border to be the real thing. It's good value for the money.

Other Restaurants. Monaco has more than 100 eating places, ranging from pizzerias to the restaurants of top hotels, but the serious gourmet will find more choice elsewhere along the Riviera. The clientele in Monaco is more interested in decor, ambience, and being seen in the right places, than in the food.

Café de Paris (M), place du Casino. This café, brasserie, drug store, bar, and newsagent was an institution, a great place to meet people, or to grab an unpretentious meal. Sadly it closed in 1987, but is due to rise again, in greater glory, in the summer of 1988.

NIGHTCLUBS

Jimmy'z, place du Casino. Jimmy'z operates from this address from September until June. In July and August it packs up and moves itself from av. Princesse-Grace (tel.

93–25–14–14), and calls itself **Jimmy'z de la Mer** (see the *Sporting Club* below). The location may be different, but the disco remains expensive and smart, and the clientele is still drawn from the elite.

Living Room, 7 av. des Spelugues (tel. 93–50–58–31). Another popular place to dance the night away. The Living Room door opens at 10 and doesn't close until well into the next day.

Navy Club, plage du Lavrotto. The Navy Club is a friendly place whose devoted admirers dance from 10:30 to dawn. Open all year, except Mondays.

Tiffany's, 3 av. des Spelugues (tel. 93–50–53–13). Just down the road from the Living Room, Tiffany's is open for the same hours. If it's possible, this one is even more crowded.

Cabaret

Cabaret du Casino, pl. du Casino (tel. 93–50–80–90). Every evening except Tuesday, September to June. Dinner-dance 9, floorshow at 11.

Loews, av. des Spelugues (tel. 93–50–65–00). **La Folie Russe** is the Loews nightspot—dinner-dance from 8:30, cabaret at 10:30. Open every evening except Monday.

Monte-Carlo Sporting Club, av. Princesse-Grace (tel. 93–30–71–71). **Jimmy'z** summer locale is here (see above), and so is **Chez Régine.** This nightlife complex, built on land infill, also has a very smart outdoor disco, **Parady'z** (if you try hard you'll get Paradise out of that!), and **La Salle des Etoiles,** with both dinner-dance and cabaret. The whole complex is open July and August, with a few days added either end. Jimmy'z and Parady'z open from 11 to the wee small hours, Salle des Etoiles from 9.

SHOPPING

Monte Carlo is the perfect place for shopping in the grand style, but don't look for bargains. All the big names are here, from Cartier to Vuitton, all the assistants speak English and all the tills are happy to accept dollars, pounds, deutschemarks, yen, and, of course, plastic. The visitor can't help feeling they'd probably accept gold ingots, too—in fact with prices like these an ingot would probably be the most appropriate currency.

EXCURSIONS

There are full-day and half-day cruises to Italy and Menton throughout the summer, and bus trips along the French and Italian Rivieras. Check with the tourist office for times and details.

It is possible to walk from Monte Carlo Beach to Cap Martin and back again in three hours, along an attractive path overlooking the sea. In the other direction, a similar path and time span will take walkers from Fontvieille to Cap d'Ail and back.

See the *From Nice to Monaco and Menton* section in the Nice chapter for interesting drives, and other suggestions for excursions.

Menton

Menton is a calm and pleasant place, with safe beaches and lemon groves, and internationally famous for its Chamber Music Festival. The mountains, which protect it without crowding it, ensure that it has its own mild microclimate, with the average temperature always a degree or so warmer than that of Nice. It calls itself the pearl of the Riviera and a pearl seems very appropriate—beautiful, respectable, and not grossly expensive.

The old town to the east, with its typically narrow streets, is only a few hundred yards from the Italian border. The western side has wider avenues and modern buildings in amongst the palace-hotels built during the great Victorian era of aristocratic tourism. Many of these grand hotels have been converted into apartments, and the majority of today's hotels fall into the (M) or (I) category. The climate, the parks and gardens, the casino, the yacht marina, and the various sporting and cultural events ensure that Menton is lively all year round—although particularly so when the wintry breezes blow Riviera visitors out of St.-Tropez.

The long stretch of beach is divided into public and private *plages*—safe for children—with lifeguards and lookout towers, all with equipment for snorkeling, sailing, windsurfing, and waterskiing.

Exploring

A good place to start is at the **Casino,** on the promenade du Soleil. Walk east along the prom, with views of the Alps on the left and the seaside cafés and beaches on the right.

At the quai Napoléon III there stands a small 17th-century fort, where Jean Cocteau, the artist, writer, and film maker, once worked. It now houses the **Cocteau Museum**—a collection of paintings which may be small in number, but are large and fantastical in theme. There are also drawings, stage sets, a tapestry, and Cocteau's engaging pebble mosaic floor of the Salamander. The fort is open Wednesdays to Sundays, mornings and afternoons, and closed public holidays.

Above the jetty is the Old Town, so Italian in style and feeling and so very different from 19th-century Menton. Climb the heart-stopping flight of steps to the wonderfully theatrical square of St.-Michel where the concerts of the Chamber Music Festival are held on warm August nights. The Baroque interior of **St.-Michel's Church**—based on the Church of the Annunciation in Genoa—is rated as highly as any in the area. It has richly decorative side chapels and fine altarpieces—and above the high altar itself, St.-Michel puts paid to the dragon. Don't miss the **Chapel of the White Penitents,** up a few steps beside the church.

More steps lead up the hill to the **Vieux Cimetière,** the old cemetery which, despite its name, dates only from Victorian times. Meditating among the tombs has a certain somber charm, lightened by the magnificent views of the Old Town and the coast. Here lie the foreigners—Russian, German, and English—who came to Menton in the hope that its mild climate would reverse the ravages of tuberculosis. The dates on the stones show that their hope was illusory, but it must have been a nice place to die. Seek out the grave of William Webb Ellis who, as his gravestone says "with a fine disregard for the rules . . . first took the ball in his arms and ran with it. . . ," thus inventing Rugby Football.

Return to the square and cut down to rue St.-Michel, a narrow pedestrian-only street lined with attractive shops, boutiques, and orange trees. Place aux Herbes, a lovely square with outdoor café and fountain, is just off rue St.-Michel, towards the sea side, and a good spot to stop for a relaxed beer en route.

Continue west along the lively and picturesque rue St.-Michel and take a right turn into the av. de la République. Here stands the **Town Hall,** the Hôtel de Ville. Inside, take a look at the room where civil marriage ceremonies are conducted. Its walls and ceiling were decorated by Jean Cocteau with suitably romantic scenes, including the distinctly inappropriate story of Orpheus and Eurydice. Open 8:30 to 12, 1:30 to 5:45, Monday to Friday.

Return to the rue St.-Michel, follow it until it becomes the av. Félix Faure and leads you to the **Bioves Gardens** behind the new casino. This formal park, with its palms and lemon trees, flowers and statues, is a fragrant reminder of the lovely things that can flourish in this gentle climate. Walk through the gardens to the **Palais d'Europe,** the old casino built in Belle Epoque style, which is now a well-equipped conference center.

Two other places which are well worth visiting lie at opposite ends of Menton. West of the Jardin Bioves is the **Palais Carnoles,** an 18th-century Italianate villa, at one time summer residence for the Prince of Monaco. The gardens are exceptionally beautiful, and inside there is an important collection of pictures. European oil paintings from the 13th to the 18th centuries hang upstairs, together with drawings and watercolors. Modern works of art are on the ground floor; Graham Sutherland, made an honorary citizen of Menton in 1968, is among those represented here. It opens mornings and afternoons and is closed Mondays, Tuesdays, and public holidays.

At the other end of the town, above the Garavan harbor, are the 14 acres of the luxuriant **Mediterranean Colombières Garden,** the lushness of the trees, shrubs, and flowering plants relieved by the occasional folly or statue, and by the belvédère with its dazzling view. The villa is partially decorated inside to an ancient Roman theme. The garden opens mornings and afternoons every day except Tuesday.

INFORMATION

- **Tourist Office.** The tourist office is located at the Palais d'Europe, av. Boyer (tel. 93-57-57-00). The staff will be able to tell you which hotels have vacancies, as well as giving out all the usual tourist information.
- **Post Code.** The post code for Menton is 06500, and must be used when writing to any Menton address.
- **Car Hire. Avis,** 9 rue Victor Hugo (tel. 93-35-50-98), and at the Gare SNCF (tel. 93-35-50-98). **Europcar,** 9 av. Thiers (tel. 93-28-21-80).

ACCESS

Menton is only about 20 miles from Nice airport. If you are hiring a car, note that the airport is very near the entrance to the expressway, which is the best and fastest route, unless you want a scenic drive. Alternatively, the airport bus goes to the railroad station, with its regular train service, or to Nice's Gare Routière where regular buses set out on the short journey to Menton.

For those traveling by train, Menton, like Nice and Monaco, is on the main line. Menton's rail station is near the town center and the tourist office. Drivers should follow the A8 expressway, and follow signs to the town center two miles from the exit.

HAPPENINGS

Lemons are grown commercially on the terraced slopes behind the town, and that happy fact is celebrated in late January or early February with the famous Lemon Fair,

La Fête du Citron. On three successive Sundays, floats decorated with tons of citrus fruit parade through the town. The Lemon Fair is followed by the orchid exhibition at the Palais d'Europe, and there are regular flower festivals throughout the summer. It's no wonder that Menton has been such a regular winner of the prize awarded to France's most flower-bedecked town.

Music lovers congregate in August for the internationally renowned Chamber Music Festival, whose concerts are held in the open in the idyllic setting of the square outside the Church of St.-Michel, where the acoustics are excellent, and the floodlighting highly dramatic.

Musical events continue in the September Festival at the Palais d'Europe, and before that the round-France sailing race ends at Menton, with a fête.

On September 29 the feast day of the town's patron, St.-Michel, is celebrated—with another fête, naturally.

LODGING

Chambord (M), 6 av. Boyer (tel. 93–35–94–19). Open all year. This a pleasant, modern hotel, has air-conditioning, and private bath and television in all rooms. It's conveniently situated next to the Palais d'Europe and the tourist office.

Prince de Galles (M), 4 av. Général de Gaulle (tel. 93–28–21–21). 68 rooms. Open all year. One of three good hotels in lovely locations right on the seafront. All the rooms in this one are well-appointed, and there is a parking lot.

Princess et Richmond (M), 617 promenade du Soleil (tel. 93–35–80–20). 43 rooms. Open from late December to early November. This is another of the sea front trio, and very comfortable with it.

Viking (M), 2 av. Général de Gaulle (tel. 93–57–95–85). 36 rooms. Open early December to early November. The third good seafront hotel, this one is right at the upper end of the (M) bracket, and can offer a swimming pool.

Globe (I), 21 av. de Verdun (tel. 93-35-73-03). 24 rooms. Open from late December to early November. The Globe is opposite the Palais d'Europe, with very satisfactory rooms and service at a distinctly bargain price.

DINING

Auberge des Santons (E), colline de l'Annonciade (tel. 93-35-94-10). Closed mid-November to mid-December. Although this restaurant is a bit out of the center, on a height near l'Annonciade Monastery, it's worth the effort of getting there for the combination of delicious *nouvelle cuisine*—cooked by master chef Bernard Simon—and a magnificent view.

Chez Mireille (M), promenade du Soleil (tel. 93-35-77-23). Usually open. There's good food, an agreeable ambience, and it's thoroughly reliable. There are 21 (M) rooms.

Le Gourmet (M), promenade du Soleil (tel. 93-57-10-22). Open Wednesday to Monday, and closed November. There are no real temples to gastronomy in Menton, but Pascal Steffan, who worked under Dominique Le Stanc in Monte Carlo, is trying to bring a more inventive touch to Menton cuisine. The restaurant is in the Casino complex, and has a delightful terrace and stylish decor.

Le Galion (I), porte de Garavan (tel. 93-35-89-73). Closed Tuesdays, and from mid-October to mid-December, and from mid-January through February. It's informal and relaxing, with a good Italian menu.

Paris-Palais (I), 2 av. Félix Faure (tel. 93-35-86-66). Closed mid-November to mid-December. Here you will find good food served in a charming restaurant with its own private garden and a wondrous view.

Nightclubs

Club 06, in the casino. The roulette and other games of chance take place in the casino itself—in Club 06, in season, you can dance the night away and watch top-class cabaret.

Excursions

The village of **Ste.-Agnès,** nestling 1,500 feet up in the mountains, is only eight miles away from Menton, and the drive there, although necessarily slow, is a scenic must. It's wise to acquire a local map which will show the way to circumnavigate Mont Agel, via **Peille**—itself a very pretty village. The road is narrow, but as it climbs the views get progressively more stunning. In spring, when the wild flowers are out, it is quite breathtaking.

The hills inland from Menton offer good walks, and the tourist office publishes a leaflet detailing 15 different rambles, to suit all energy levels.

Visiting Italy

Menton is right on the frontier between France and Italy and it's very easy to visit the Italian towns of Ventimiglia and San Remo by train, bus, or car.

One of the most exciting times to go is on a Friday, when the people of Menton flock to the busy flower market at **Ventimiglia.** If you decide to go too, use public transport because parking spaces are virtually nonexistent on market days. Don't neglect to wander round the town itself, which has plenty of cheerful, inexpensive restaurants and a supermarket, **Standa,** right in the center, full of cheap and colorful mass-produced goods, some local, some from the Far East.

American and British subjects will need their passports to cross the frontier, and there are restrictions on bringing back goods to France, particularly alcohol and tobacco.

INDEX

Map references are found in **bold**.

Accommodations. *See* Hotels
African Queen (Beaulieu), 103
Agay, 35–36
Air travel, 15, 92
Albert's Bar (Nice), 97
Alexandra (Monaco), 115
Alps, 100–101
Ane Rouge (Nice), 96
Annot, 101
Antibes, 5, 63–66, **65**
  accommodations in, 70–71
  climate in, 12–13
  excursions from, 76–81
  information sources for, 69
  restaurants in, 73
  seasonal events in, 69–70
  shopping in, 76
Armandier de Mougins, L' (Mougins), 60
Au Bec Fin (Cannes), 56
Auberge de l'Estérel (Juan-les-Pins), 72, 75
Auberge du Jarrier, l' (Biot), 77
Auberge des Santons (Menton), 124
Auron, 101
Automboiles, 16–17. *See also* rentals cars
  in Cannes, 50
  in Mandelieu-La Napoule, 39
  in Menton, 122
  in Nice, 92, 102–104
  in St.-Tropez, 27

Bacon (Cap d'Antibes), 73–74
Balmoral (Monaco), 115
Banks, 11
Baraale (Nice), 97
Beaches, 3–4
  in Cannes, 46–47
  in Menton, 119–120
  in Monaco, 111
  in Nice, 83–84
  near St.-Tropez, 24–26
Beaulieu, 102–103
Beau Séjour (Cannes), 54
Bec Rouge (Monaco), 115
Belles Rives, Les (Juan-les-Pins), 71–72, 74
Bioes Gardens (Menton), 121
Biot, 76–77
Bistrot d'Antoine, Le (Nice), 98
Boats
  in Antibes, 69
  in Cannes, 48–50
  to Les Iles de Lérins, 59
  in Monaco, 112
  in Nice, 91

127

INDEX

Boats (*continued*)
  in St.-Tropez, 27
Bonne Auberge, La
  (Antibes), 73
Boulevard de la Croisette
  (Cannes), 46, 47
Bureau, Le (Juan-les-Pins),
  75
Buses, 16, 108
Byblos (St.-Tropez), 28–29

Cabaret, in Monaco, 117
Café des Arts (St.-Tropez), 24
Café de Paris (Monaco), 116
Cagnard, Le (Villeneuve-
  Loubet), 79
Cannes, 5, 46–48, **49**
  accommodations in, 52–55
  excursions from, 59–62
  history of, 45–46
  information sources for,
    48–50
  nightclubs in, 57–58
  restaurants in, 55–57
  seasonal events in, 51
  shopping in, 58–59
  transportation to, 50
Cap d'Antibes, 63, 67–68.
  See also Antibes
  accommodations in, 71
  restaurants in, 73–74
Carnival (Nice), 93
Casinos
  in Cannes, 57
  invention of, 2, 106
  in Menton, 121
  in Monaco, 107, 108
  in Nice, 99
Chabichou, Le (St.-Tropez),
  30–31
Chamber Music Festival
  (Menton), 119, 123
Chambord (Menton), 123
Chantecler (Nice), 96–97
Chapel de l'Annunciation
  (Nice), 86

Chapelle du Rosaire (Vence),
  81
Château (Villeneuve-
  Loubet), 78–79
Château Grimaldi (Antibes),
  66
Chez Loulou (Mandelieu-La
  Napoule), 41
Chez Mireille (Menton), 124
Church of the Immaculate
  Conception (Antibes),
  64
Citadel (St.-Tropez), 24
Climate, 11–14
Coco Beach (Nice), 97
Cocteau Museum (Menton),
  120
Colline du Château, la
  (Nice), 87
Colombe d'Or (St.-Paul-de-
  Vence), 79
Condamine, La (Monaco),
  105
Costs, 10–11
  of hotels, 17–18
  of restaurants, 18
Côte d'Azur, 2
Coupole (Monaco), 115
Cours Saleya (Nice), 86
Credit cards, 11
Crystal, Le (Juan-les-Pins),
  75
Currency, 11
Customs, 14–15

Dauphins Verts, Les
  (Cannes), 54
Dents de la Mer, Les (Nice),
  97
Digne, 101
Domaine d'Olival, Le
  (Mandelieu-La
  Napoule), 40
Dominique le Stanc
  (Monaco), 116
Durante (Nice), 95

INDEX

Eglise-St.-Jacques (Nice), 86
Eglise-St.-Martin-St.-Augustin (Nice), 87
Entertainment
  in Cannes, 57–58
  in Juan-les-Pins, 75
  in Mandelieu-La Napoule, 42
  in Menton, 125
  in Monaco, 116–117
  in Nice, 99
  in St.-Tropez, 29, 31–32
Ermitage (St.-Tropez), 30
Ermitage du Riou (Mandelieu-La Napoule), 40–41
Eze, 104

Ferme de Mougins, La (Mougins), 60–61
Fernand Léger Museum (Biot), 77
Festival (hotel; Cannes), 54
Feu Follet, Le (Mougins), 61
Film Festival (Cannes), 51
Fimotel Neptune Antibes, 72
Fishing, 42
Florian (Nice), 97
Fondation Maeght (St.-Paul-de-Vence), 80
Fontvieille (Monaco), 105
Foundation Henry Clews (Mandelieu-La Napoule), 38
Foundation Rothschild (Villefranche), 102
Fouquets, Le (Cannes), 53
Fragonard Villa Museum (Grasse), 62
France
  information sources for, 9–10
  passports, visas and customs for, 14–15
  refunds of taxes in, 19–20
Fréjus, 34

Galerie de Malcologie (Nice), 86
Galion, Le (Menton), 124
Gardiole, La (Cap d'Antibes), 71
Giardino, Il (Antibes), 73
Globe (Menton), 124
Golf, 42–43
Gorille, Le (St.-Tropez), 23
Gourmet, Le (Menton), 124
Gourmet Lorrain (Nice), 95–96, 98
Grand Café de Turin (Nice), 87, 98–99
Grasse, 61–62
Grille (Monaco), 115

Helicopters, 91, 92, 112
Horse riding, 43
Hôtel du Cap d'Antibes, 71
Hôtel Gonnet et de la Reine (Cannes), 54
Hôtel Gray d'Albion (Cannes), 52–53, 55
Hôtel Negresco (Nice), 11, 84, 94, 96–98
Hôtel de Paris (Monaco), 114–115
Hotels
  in Agay, 35–36
  in Antibes and Juan-les-Pins, 70–73
  in Cannes, 52–55
  in Mandelieu-La Napoule, 40–41
  in Menton, 119, 123–124
  in Monaco, 107–110, 114–115
  in Nice, 84, 94–96
  in Ste.-Maxine, 34
  in St.-Paul-de-Vence, 79–80
  in St.-Tropez, 28–30
  in Villeneuve-Loubet, 79
Hôtel St.-Christophe (Agay), 35–36

Hyères, Les Iles d' (Les Iles d'Or), 32–33

Ibis (Sophia Antipolis), 73
Information sources, 9–10
 for Antibes and Juan-les-Pins, 69
 for Cannes, 48
 for Mandelieu-La Napoule, 38
 for Menton, 122
 for Monaco, 106, 112
 for Nice, 91, 96
 for St.-Tropez, 26
 for skiing in Alps, 101
 for Vence, 81
International Film Festival (Cannes), 46, 51
Isola 2000 (ski resort), 101
Italy, 125–126

Jardin Albert I (Nice), 83
Jardin Exotique (Eze), 104
Jardin Thuret (Cap d'Antibes), 68
Juana (Juan-les-Pins), 72, 74–75
Juan-les-Pins, 5, 63–64, **65**, 67. *See also* Antibes
 accommodations in, 71–72
 information sources for, 69
 nightclubs in, 75
 restaurants in, 74–75
 seasonal events in, 69–70

Lauriers, Les (St.-Tropez), 30
Lérins, Les Iles de, 59
Levant, Ile du, 33
Loews (Mandelieu-La Napoule), 40
Loews (Monaco), 114
Logis Sant Estello (Mandelieu-La Napoule), 41
Louis XV (Monaco), 114–116

Madone, La (Cannes), 54
Mandelieu, 34–36
Mandelieu-La Napoule, 4–5, 37–38
 accommodations in, 40–41
 excursions from, 43–44
 restaurants in, 41–42
 seasonal events in, 39–40
 transportation to, 39
Maphotel Golf de Valescure (Ste.-Maxine), 34
Martineland (near Antibes), 76
Martinez (Cannes), 52, 55–56
Mas Djoliba (Antibes), 70
Mas d'Artigny (St.-Paul-de-Vence), 80
Massif de l'Estérel, 34
Mediterranean Colombières Garden (Menton), 121–122
Menton, 119–123
 accommodations in, 123–124
 excursions from, 125–126
 from Nice to, 102–104
 restaurants in, 124–125
Merande, La (Nice), 98
Mére Besson, La (Cannes), 56
Meridien (Nice), 94
Métropole, La (Beaulieu), 103
Mimosas, Les (Juan-les-Pins), 72
Monaco, 2, 6, 105–111, **109**
 accommodations in, 114–115
 excursions from, 118
 helicopters to, 91, 92
 information sources for, 112
 from Nice to, 102–104
 nightclubs in, 116–117
 restaurants in, 115–116
 seasonal events in, 113

shopping in, 117–118
transportation to, 112–113
Money, 11
Monte Carlo. *See* Monaco
Motel Axa (Cap d'Antibes), 71
Mougins, 60–61
Moulin de Mougins, Le (Moguins), 60
Musée de l'Annonciade (St.-Tropez), 23
Musée Archéologique (Antibes), 66
Musée des Beaux-Arts, La (Nice), 90
Musée Chagall, 88
Musée Escoffier (Villeneuve-Loubet), 78
Musée de la Maritime (St.-Tropez), 24
Musée Masséna (Nice), 84
Musée Matisse (Nice), 89
Musée Naval, le (Nice), 87
Musée Naval et Napoleonien (Cap d'Antibes), 68
Musée Terra Amata (Nice), 90–91
Museum of Prehistoric Anthropology (Monaco), 111
Museums
 in Antibes, 66
 in Cap d'Antibes, 68
 Fernand Léger (Biot), 77
 in Grasse, 62
 in Menton, 120
 in Monaco, 110–111
 in Nice, 84, 86–91
 in St.-Paul-de-Vence, 80
 in St.-Tropez, 23, 24
 in Villeneuve-Loubet, 78–79

Napoule, La. *See* Mandelieu-La Napoule
Nice, 5–6, 83–91, **85**
 accommodations in, 94–96

from Antibes to, 77–78
cuisine of, 7–8
excursions from, 100–104
history of, 82–83
information sources for, 91
Monaco and, 106–107
nightclubs in, 99
restaurants in, 96–99
seasonal events in, 93
shopping in, 99–100
transportation to, 92
transportation to Monaco from, 112
Nightlife. *See* Entertainment
Notre-Dame-de-l'Assumption (Nice), 90
Novotel (Sophia Antipolis), 72–73
Novotel Montfleury (Cannes), 54

Oasis, L' (Mandelieu-La Napoule), 41–42
Observatory (Cannes), 48
Oceanography Museum and Aquarium (Monaco), 110–111
Orangerie, l' (Cannes), 56

Palais Carnoles (Menton), 121
Palais d'Europe (Menton), 121
Palais Lascaris (Nice), 86–87
Palm Beach Casino (Cannes), 57
Palme d'Or (Cannes), 55–56
Palmiers, Les (St.-Tropez), 30
Paris-Palais (Menton), 124
Passports, 14, 126
Pavillon Eden Roc (Cap d'Antibes), 74
Peille, 125
Pérouse, La (Nice), 94–95
Petite Maison Ferrier, La (Nice), 98

Place des Lices (place Carnot; St.-Tropez), 24
Place Masséna (Nice), 83, 84, 88
Plage du Larvotto (beach, Monaco), 111
Plateau de la Garoupe (Cap d'Antibes), 68
Plateau-St.-Martin, 103–104
Poéle d'Or, La (Cannes), 56
Polpetta (Monaco), 116
Porquerolles, Ile de, 32–33
Port-Cros, Ile de, 33
Port Grimaud, 26
Préjoly, Le (St.-Vallier-de-Thiey), 62
Prince de Galles (Menton), 123
Prince's Palace (Monaco), 110
Princess et Richmond (Menton), 123
Promenade des Anglais (Nice), 83
Pullman (Nice), 95

Rental cars
  in Antibes and Juan-les-Pins, 69
  in Cannes, 48
  in Mandelieu-La Napoule, 38
  in Menton, 122
  in Monaco, 112
  in Nice, 91
  in St.-Tropez, 27
Résidence de la Pinede (St.-Tropez), 29
Restaurant du Port (Monaco), 116
Restaurants
  in Antibes and Juan-les-Pins, 73–75
  in Beaulieu, 103
  in Biot, 77
  in Cannes, 55–57
  cuisine in, 6–8
  information sources for, 9–10
  in Mandelieu-La Napoule, 41–42
  in Menton, 124
  in Monaco, 114–116
  in Nice, 94, 96–99
  in Port Grimaud, 26
  in St.-Tropez, 23, 30–31
  in Vence, 81
  prices in, 18
Riviera
  climate on, 11–14
  history of, 1–2
  prices on, 10–11
  transportation to, 15–17
Rocher, le (Monaco), 105
Roquebrune-Cap-Martin, 103
Rosaire, La (Vence), 81
Rostang, Jo and Philippe, 73
Rotonde, La (Nice), 97–98
Royal (hotel; Antibes), 70
Royal Gray (Cannes), 55
Russian Orthodox Cathedral (Nice), 90

Ste.-Agnès, 125
St.-Honorat, 59
Ste.-Marguerite, 59
Ste.-Maxime, 34
St.-Michel's Church (Menton), 120
St.-Paul-de-Vence, 79–80
St.-Raphael, 34
St.-Tropez, 4, 23–26, **25**
  accommodations in, 28–30
  excursions from, 32–36
  history of, 21–22
  information sources for, 26–27
  nightclubs in, 31–32
  restaurants in, 30–31
  shopping in, 32
  transportation to, 27–28
St.-Vallier-de-Thiey, 62
Sanctuaire de la Garoupe (Cap d'Antibes), 68
Seafood, 7
Seasonal events
  in Antibes and Juan-les-

INDEX

Pins, 69–70
Cannes Film Festival, 51
in Mandelieu-La Napoule, 39–40
in Menton, 122–123
in Monaco, 113
in Nice, 93
in St.-Tropez, 28
Sénequier (St.-Tropez), 23
Shopping, 19
in Antibes and Juan-les-Pins, 76
in Cannes, 58–59
in Mandelieu-La Napoule, 42
in Monaco, 117–118
in Mougins, 61
in Nice, 88, 99–100
in St.-Tropez, 32
Siesta, Le (Juan-les-Pins), 75
Skiing, 101
Société des Bains de Mer (casino; Monte Carlo), 106, 107
Sofitel-Splendid (Nice), 95
Sol e Mar (Agay), 35
Sophia Antipolis, 72–73
Suisse (hotel; Nice), 96

Tartane, La (Port Grimaud), 26
Tartane, La (St.-Tropez), 30
Taxes, 19–20
Tennis, 43
Terrasse, La (Juan-les-Pins), 74–75
Tipping, 19
Trains, 15–16
to Alps, 100–101
to Monaco, 112–113
to Nice, 92

Transportation
to Antibes and Juan-les-Pins, 69
to Cannes, 50
to Les Iles d'Hyères, 33
to Mandelieu-La Napoule, 39
to Menton, 122
to Monaco, 112–113
to Nice, 92
to Riviera, 15–17
to St.-Tropez, 27
Trophée des Alpes, La (La Turbie), 104
Tropical Gardens (Monaco), 111
Turbie, La, 104

Valberg, 101
Value-added tax (VAT), 19–20
Vence, 80–81
Ventimiglia (Italy), 125–126
Victoria (Nice), 95
Vielle Ville, la, 80–81
Vieux Cimetière (Menton), 120–121
Viking (Menton), 123
Villa Kérylos (Beaulieu), 102–103
Villefranche, 102
Villeneuve-Loubet, 78–79
Visas, 14

Wagram (Cannes), 54–55
Waterskiing, 50
Water sports, 43
Windsurfing, 50
Wines, 8

Yaca, Le (St.-Tropez), 29–30

FODOR'S TRAVEL GUIDES

Here is a complete list of Fodor's Travel Guides, available in current editions; most are also available in a British edition published by Hodder & Stoughton.

U.S. GUIDES

Alaska
American Cities (Great Travel Values)
Arizona including the Grand Canyon
Atlantic City & the New Jersey Shore
Boston
California
Cape Cod & the Islands of Martha's Vineyard & Nantucket
Carolinas & the Georgia Coast
Chesapeake
Chicago
Colorado
Dallas/Fort Worth
Disney World & the Orlando Area (Fun in)
Far West
Florida
Fort Worth (see Dallas)
Galveston (see Houston)
Georgia (see Carolinas)
Grand Canyon (see Arizona)
Greater Miami & the Gold Coast
Hawaii
Hawaii (Great Travel Values)
Houston & Galveston
I-10: California to Florida
I-55: Chicago to New Orleans
I-75: Michigan to Florida
I-80: San Francisco to New York
I-95: Maine to Miami
Jamestown (see Williamsburg)
Las Vegas including Reno & Lake Tahoe (Fun in)
Los Angeles & Nearby Attractions
Martha's Vineyard (see Cape Cod)
Maui (Fun in)
Nantucket (see Cape Cod)
New England
New Jersey (see Atlantic City)
New Mexico
New Orleans
New Orleans (Fun in)
New York City
New York City (Fun in)
New York State
Orlando (see Disney World)
Pacific North Coast
Philadelphia
Reno (see Las Vegas)
Rockies
San Diego & Nearby Attractions
San Francisco (Fun in)
San Francisco plus Marin County & the Wine Country
The South
Texas
U.S.A.
Virgin Islands (U.S. & British)
Virginia
Waikiki (Fun in)
Washington, D.C.
Williamsburg, Jamestown & Yorktown

FOREIGN GUIDES

Acapulco (see Mexico City)
Acapulco (Fun in)
Amsterdam
Australia, New Zealand & the South Pacific
Austria
The Bahamas
The Bahamas (Fun in)
Barbados (Fun in)
Beijing, Guangzhou & Shanghai
Belgium & Luxembourg
Bermuda
Brazil
Britain (Great Travel Values)
Canada
Canada (Great Travel Values)
Canada's Maritime Provinces plus Newfoundland & Labrador
Cancún, Cozumel, Mérida & the Yucatán
Caribbean
Caribbean (Great Travel Values)
Central America
Copenhagen (see Stockholm)
Cozumel (see Cancún)
Eastern Europe
Egypt
Europe
Europe (Budget)
France
France (Great Travel Values)
Germany: East & West
Germany (Great Travel Values)
Great Britain
Greece
Guangzhou (see Beijing)
Helsinki (see Stockholm)
Holland
Hong Kong & Macau
Hungary
India, Nepal & Sri Lanka
Ireland
Israel
Italy
Italy (Great Travel Values)
Jamaica (Fun in)
Japan
Japan (Great Travel Values)
Jordan & the Holy Land
Kenya
Korea
Labrador (see Canada's Maritime Provinces)
Lisbon
Loire Valley
London
London (Fun in)
London (Great Travel Values)
Luxembourg (see Belgium)
Macau (see Hong Kong)
Madrid
Mazatlan (see Mexico's Baja)
Mexico
Mexico (Great Travel Values)
Mexico City & Acapulco
Mexico's Baja & Puerto Vallarta, Mazatlan, Manzanillo, Copper Canyon
Montreal (Fun in)
Munich
Nepal (see India)
New Zealand
Newfoundland (see Canada's Maritime Provinces)
1936 . . . on the Continent
North Africa
Oslo (see Stockholm)
Paris
Paris (Fun in)
People's Republic of China
Portugal
Province of Quebec
Puerto Vallarta (see Mexico's Baja)
Reykjavik (see Stockholm)
Rio (Fun in)
The Riviera (Fun on)
Rome
St. Martin/St. Maarten (Fun in)
Scandinavia
Scotland
Shanghai (see Beijing)
Singapore
South America
South Pacific
Southeast Asia
Soviet Union
Spain
Spain (Great Travel Values)
Sri Lanka (see India)
Stockholm, Copenhagen, Oslo, Helsinki & Reykjavik
Sweden
Switzerland
Sydney
Tokyo
Toronto
Turkey
Vienna
Yucatán (see Cancún)
Yugoslavia

SPECIAL-INTEREST GUIDES

Bed & Breakfast Guide: North America
Royalty Watching
Selected Hotels of Europe
Selected Resorts and Hotels of the U.S.
Ski Resorts of North America
Views to Dine by around the World

AVAILABLE AT YOUR LOCAL BOOKSTORE OR WRITE TO FODOR'S TRAVEL PUBLICATIONS, INC., 201 EAST 50th STREET, NEW YORK, NY 10022.